5th Workshop on Vision and Language (VL'16)

Held at ACL 2016

Berlin, Germany
12 August 2016

ISBN: 978-1-5108-2763-9

ACL 2016

5th Workshop on Vision and Language
(VL'16)

Proceedings of the Workshop

August 12, 2016

This workshop is supported by ICT COST Action IC1307, the European Network on Integrating Vision and Language (iV&L Net): Combining Computer Vision and Language Processing For Advanced Search, Retrieval, Annotation and Description of Visual Data.

Introduction

The Fifth Workshop on Vision and Language 2016 (VL'16) took place in Berlin on the 12th August 2016, as part of ACL'16. The workshop is organised by the European Network on Integrating Vision and Language which is funded as a European COST Action. The VL workshops have the general aims: 1. to provide a forum for reporting and discussing planned, ongoing and completed research that involves both language and vision; and 2. to enable NLP and computer vision researchers to meet, exchange ideas, expertise and technology, and form new research partnerships.

The call for papers for VL'16 elicited a good number of submissions, each of which was peer-reviewed by three members of the programme committee. The interest in the workshop from leading NLP and computer vision researchers and the quality of submissions was high, so we aimed to be as inclusive as possible within the practical constraints of the workshop. In the end, we accepted five submissions as long papers, and eight as short papers. The resulting workshop programme packed a lot of exciting content into one day. We were delighted to be able to include in the programme a keynote presentation by Yejin Choi, University of Washington.

We would like to thank all the people who have contributed to the organisation and delivery of this workshop: the authors who submitted such high quality papers; the programme committee for their prompt and effective reviewing; our keynote speaker; the ACL 2016 organising committee, especially the workshops chairs; the participants in the workshop; and future readers of these proceedings for your shared interest in this exciting new area of research.

August 2016,
Anja Belz, Erkut Erdem, Krystian Mikolajczyk and Katerina Pastra

Organizers:

Anya Belz, University of Brighton, UK
Erkut Erdem, Hacettepe University, Turkey
Krystian Mikolajczyk, Imperial College London, UK
Katerina Pastra, Cognitive Systems Research Institute, Greece

Program Committee:

Yannis Aloimonos, University of Maryland, US
Marco Baroni, University of Trento, Italy
Raffaella Bernardi, University of Trento, Italy
Ruken Cakici, Middle East Technical University, Turkey
Luisa Coheur, University of Lisbon, Portugal
Pinar Duygulu Sah'n, Hacettepe University, Turkey
Desmond Elliott, University of Amsterdam, Netherlands
Aykut Erdem, Hacettepe University, Turkey
Jordi Gonzalez, Autonomous University of Barcelona, Spain
Lewis Griffin, UCL, UK
David Hogg, University of Leeds, UK
Nazli Ikizler-Cinbis, Hacettepe University, Turkey
John Kelleher, UCD, Ireland
Frank Keller, University of Edinburgh, UK
Mirella Lapata, University of Edinburgh, UK
Fei Fei Li, Stanford University, US
Margaret Mitchell, Microsoft Research, US
Sien Moens, University of Leuven, Belgium
Francesc Moreno-Noguer, CSIC-UPC, Spain
Adrian Muscat, University of Malta, Malta
Ram Nevatia, University of Southern California, US
Barbara Plank, CST, University of Copenhagen, Denmark
Arnau Ramisa, INRIA Rhone-Alpes, France
Richard Socher, MetaMind Inc, US
Tinne Tuytelaars, University of Leuven, Belgium
Josiah Wang, University of Sheffield, UK
Fei Yan, University of Surrey, UK

Invited Speaker:

Yejin Choi, University of Washington, US

Table of Contents

Workshop Program

Friday, August 12, 2016

9:00–9:30   *Opening Remarks*

9:30–10:00   *Automatic Annotation of Structured Facts in Images*
Mohamed Elhoseiny, Scott Cohen, Walter Chang, Brian Price and Ahmed Elgammal

10:00–10:30   *Combining Lexical and Spatial Knowledge to Predict Spatial Relations between Objects in Images*
Manuela Hürlimann and Johan Bos

10:30–11:00   *Coffee Break*

11:00–12:00   ***Invited talk: Yejin Choi***

12:00–12:30   *Focused Evaluation for Image Description with Binary Forced-Choice Tasks*
Micah Hodosh and Julia Hockenmaier

12:30–14:00   *Lunch Break*

14:00–14:30   *Leveraging Captions in the Wild to Improve Object Detection*
Mert Kilickaya, Nazli Ikizler-Cinbis, Erkut Erdem and Aykut Erdem

14:30–15:30   ***Quick-fire presentations for posters (5mins each)***

15:30–16:00   *Coffee Break*

16:00–17:30   *Poster Session*

     Natural Language Descriptions of Human Activities Scenes: Corpus Generation and Analysis
Nouf Alharbi and Yoshihiko Gotoh

     Interactively Learning Visually Grounded Word Meanings from a Human Tutor
Yanchao Yu, Arash Eshghi and Oliver Lemon

Automatic Annotation of Structured Facts in Images

Mohamed Elhoseiny[1,2]**, Scott Cohen**[1]**, Walter Chang**[1]**, Brian Price**[1]**, Ahmed Elgammal**[2]

[1]Adobe Research   [2]Department of Computer Science, Rutgers University

Abstract

Motivated by the application of fact-level image understanding, we present an automatic method for data collection of structured visual facts from images with captions. Example structured facts include attributed objects (e.g., <flower, red>), actions (e.g., <baby, smile>), interactions (e.g., <man, walking, dog>), and positional information (e.g., <vase, on, table>). The collected annotations are in the form of fact-image pairs (e.g.,<man, walking, dog> and an image region containing this fact). With a language approach, the proposed method is able to collect hundreds of thousands of visual fact annotations with accuracy of 83% according to human judgment. Our method automatically collected more than 380,000 visual fact annotations and more than 110,000 unique visual facts from images with captions and localized them in images in less than one day of processing time on standard CPU platforms. We will make the data publically available.

1 Introduction

People generally acquire visual knowledge by exposure to both visual facts and to semantic or language-based representations of these facts, e.g., by seeing an image of "a person petting dog" and observing this visual fact associated with its language representation . In this work, we focus on methods for collecting structured facts that we define as structures that provide attributes about an object, and/or the actions and interactions this object may have with other objects. We introduce the idea of automatically collecting annotations for second order visual facts and third order vi-

sual facts where second order facts <S,P> are attributed objects (e.g., <S: car, P: red>) and single-frame actions (e.g., <S: person, P: jumping>), and third order facts specify interactions (i.e., <boy, petting, dog>). This structure is helpful for designing machine learning algorithms that learn deeper image semantics from caption data and allow us to model the relationships between facts. In order to enable such a setting, we need to collect these structured fact annotations in the form of (language view, visual view) pairs (e.g., <baby, sitting on, chair> as the language view and an image with this fact as a visual view) to train models.

(Chen et al., 2013) showed that visual concepts, from a predefined ontology, can be learned by querying the web about these concepts using image-web search engines. More recently, (Divvala et al., 2014) presented an approach to learn concepts related to a particular object by querying the web with Google-N-gram data that has the concept name. There are three limitations to these approaches. (1) It is difficult to define the space of visual knowledge and then search for it. It is further restricting to define it based on a predefined ontology such as (Chen et al., 2013) or a particular object such as (Divvala et al., 2014). (2) Using image search is not reliable to collect data for concepts with few images on the web. These methods assume that the top retrieved examples by image-web search are positive examples and that there are images available that are annotated with the searched concept. (3) These concepts/facts are not structured and hence annotations lacks information like "jumping" is the action part in <person, jumping >, or "man' and "horse" are interacting in <person, riding, horse >. This structure is important for deeper understanding of visual data, which is one of the main motivations of this work.

The problems in the prior work motivate us to propose a method to automatically annotate struc-

1

Proceedings of the 5th Workshop on Vision and Language, pages 1–9,
Berlin, Germany, August 12 2016. ©2016 Association for Computational Linguistics

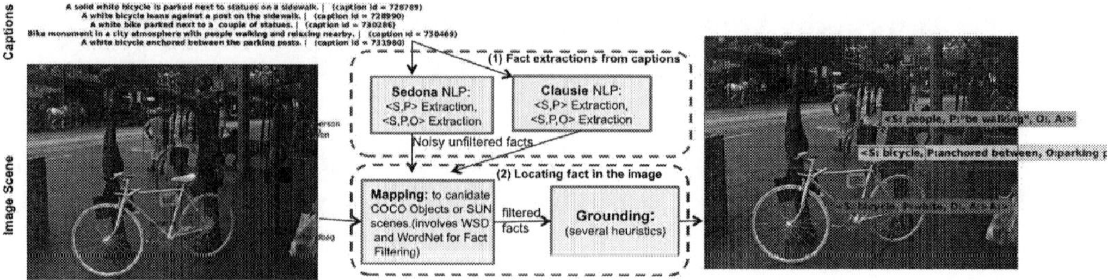

Figure 1: Structured Fact Automatic Annotation

tured facts by processing image caption data since facts in image captions are highly likely to be located in the associated images. We show that a large quantity of high quality structured visual facts could be extracted from caption datasets using natural language processing methods. Caption writing is free-form and an easier task for crowd-sourcing workers than labeling second- and third-order tasks, and such free-form descriptions are readily available in existing image caption datasets. We focused on collecting facts from the MS COCO image caption dataset (Lin et al., 2014) and the newly collected Flickr30K entities (Plummer et al., 2015). We automatically collected more than 380,000 structured fact annotations in high quality from both the 120,000 MS COCO scenes and 30,000 Flickr30K scenes.

The main contribution of this paper is an accurate, automatic, and efficient method for extraction of structured fact visual annotations from image-caption datasets, as illustrated in Fig. 1. Our approach (1) extracts facts from captions associated with images and then (2) localizes the extracted facts in the image. For fact extraction from captions, We propose a new method called *SedonaNLP* for fact extraction to fill gaps in existing fact extraction from sentence methods like Clausie (Del Corro and Gemulla, 2013). SedonaNLP produces more facts than Clausie, especially <subject,attribute> facts, and thus enables collecting more visual annotations than using Clausie alone. The final set of automatic annotations are the set of successfully localized facts in the associated images. We show that these facts are extracted with more than 80% accuracy according to human judgment.

2 Motivation

Our goal by proposing this automatic method is to generate language&vision annotations at the fact-level to help study language&vision for the sake of structured understanding of visual facts. Existing systems already work on relating captions directly to the whole image such as (Karpathy et al., 2014; Kiros et al., 2015; Vinyals et al., 2015; Xu et al., 2015; Mao et al., 2015; Antol et al., 2015; Malinowski et al., 2015; Ren et al., 2015). This gives rise to a key question about our work: why it is useful to collect such a large quantity of structured facts compared to caption-level systems?

We illustrate the difference between caption-level learning fact-level learning that motivates this work by the example in Fig 1. Caption-level learning systems correlate captions like those on top of Fig. 1(top-left) to the whole image that includes all objects. Structured Fact-level learning systems are instead fed with localized annotations for each fact extracted form the image caption; see in Fig. 1(right), Fig. 6, and 7 in Sec. 6. Fact level annotations are less confusing training data than sentences because they provide more precise information for both the language and the visual views. **(1)** From the language view, the annotations we generate is precise to list a particular fact (e.g., <bicycle,parked between, parking posts>). **(2)** From the visual view, it provide the bounding box of this fact; see Fig 1. **(3)** A third unique part about our annotations is the structure: e.g., <bicycle,parked between, parking posts> instead of "a bicycle parked between parking posts".

Our collected data has been used to develop methods that learn hundreds of thousands of image facts, as we introduced and studied in (Elhoseiny et al., 2016a). The results shows that fact-level learning is superior compared to caption-level learning like (Kiros et al., 2015), as shown in Table 4 in (Elhoseiny et al., 2016a) (16.39% accuracy versus 3.48% for (Kiros et al., 2015)). It further shows the value of the associated structure in the (16.39% accuracy versus 8.1%) in Table 4(Elhoseiny et al., 2016a)). Similar results also shown on a smaller scale in Table 3 in (Elhoseiny et al.,

2016a).

3 Approach Overview

We propose a two step automatic annotation of structured facts: (i) Extraction of structured fact from captions, and (ii) Localization of these facts in images. First, the captions associated with the given image are analyzed to extract sets of clauses that are considered as candidate <S,P>, and <S,P,O> facts.

Captions can provide a tremendous amount of information to image understanding systems. However, developing NLP systems to accurately and completely extract structured knowledge from free-form text is an open problem. We extract structured facts using two methods: Clausie (Del Corro and Gemulla, 2013) and Sedona(detailed later in Sec 4); also see Fig 1. We found Clausie (Del Corro and Gemulla, 2013) missed many visual facts in the captions which motivated us to develop Sedona to fill this gap as detailed in Sec. 4.

Second, we localize these facts within the image (see Fig. 1). The successfully located facts in the images are saved as fact-image annotations that could be used to train visual perception models to learn attributed objects, actions, and interactions. We managed to collect 380.409 high-quality second- and third-order fact annotations (146,515 from Flickr30K Entities, 157,122 from the MS COCO training set, and 76,772 from the MS COCO validation set). We present statistics of the automatically collected facts in the Experiments section. Note that the process of localizing facts in an image is constrained by information in the dataset.

For MS COCO, the dataset contains object annotations for about 80 different objects as provided by the training and validation sets. Although this provides abstract information about objects in each image (e.g., "person"), it is usually mentioned in different ways in the caption. For the "person" object, "man", "girl", "kid", or "child" could instead appear in the caption. In order to locate second- and third-order facts in images, we started by defining visual entities. For the MS COCO dataset (Lin et al., 2014), we define a visual entity as any noun that is either (1) one of the MS COCO dataset objects, (2) a noun in the WordNet ontology (Miller, 1995; Leacock and Chodorow, 1998) that is an immediate or indirect hyponym of one of the MS COCO objects (since WordNet is

searchable by a sense and not a word, we perform word sense disambiguation on the sentences using a state-of-the-art method (Zhong and Ng, 2010)), or (3) one of scenes the SUN dataset (Xiao et al., 2010) (e.g., a "restaurant"). We expect visual entities to appear either in the S or the O part (if exists) of a candidate fact. This allows us to then localize facts for images in the MS COCO dataset. Given a candidate third-order fact, we first try to assign each S and O to one of the visual entities. If S and O elements are not visual entities, then the fact is ignored. Otherwise, the facts are processed by several heuristics, detailed in Sec 5. For instance, our method takes into account that grounding the plural "men" in the fact <S:men, P: chasing, O: soccer ball > may require the union of multiple "man" bounding boxes.

In the Flickr30K Entities dataset (Plummer et al., 2015), the bounding box annotations are presented as phrase labels for sentences (for each phrase in a caption that refers to an entity in the scene). A visual entity is considered to be a phrase with a bounding box annotation or one of the SUN scenes. Several heuristics were developed and applied to collect these fact annotations, e.g. grounding a fact about a scene to the entire image; detailed in Sec 5.

4 Fact Extraction from Captions

We extract facts from captions using Clausie (Del Corro and Gemulla, 2013) and our proposed SedonaNLP system. In contrast to Clausie, we address several challenging linguistic issues by evolving our NLP pipeline to: 1) correct many common spelling and punctuation mistakes, 2) resolve word sense ambiguity within clauses, and 3) learn a common spatial preposition lexicon (e.g., "next_to", "on_top_of", "in_front_of") that consists of over 110 such terms, as well as a lexicon of over two dozen collection phrase adjectives (e.g., "group_of", "bunch_of", "crowd_of", "herd_of"). For our purpose, these strategies allowed us to extract more interesting structured facts that Clausie fails at which include (1) more discrimination between single versus plural terms, (2) extracting positional facts (e.g., next_to). Additionally, SedonaNLP produces attribute facts that we denote as <S, A>; see Fig 4. Similar to some existing systems OpenNLP (Baldridge, 2014) and ClearNLP (Choi, 2014), the SedonaNLP

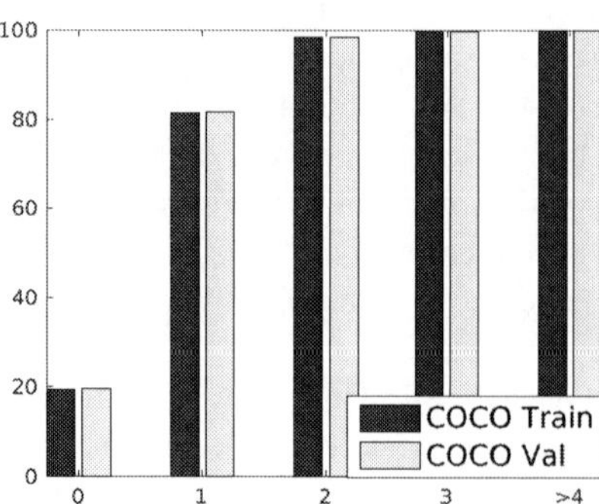

Figure 3: Accumulative Percentage of SP and SPO facts in COCO 2014 captions as number of verbs increases

platform also performs many common NLP tasks: e.g., sentence segmentation, tokenization, part-of-speech tagging, named entity extraction, chunking, dependency and constituency-based parsing, and coreference resolution. SedonaNLP itself employs both open-source components such as NLTK and WordNet, as well as internally-developed annotation algorithms for POS and clause tagging. These tasks are used to create more advanced functions such as structured fact annotation of images via semantic triple extraction. In our work, we found SedonaNLP and Clausie to be complementary for producing a set of candidate facts for possible localization in the image that resulted in successful annotations.

Varying degrees of success have been achieved in extracting and representing structured triples from sentences using <subject, predicate, object> triples. For instance, (Rusu et al., 2007) describe a basic set of methods based on traversing the parse graphs generated by various commonly available parsers. Larger scale text mining methods for learning structured facts for question answering have been developed in the IBM Watson PRISMATIC framework (Fan et al., 2010). While parsers such as CoreNLP (Manning et al., 2014) are available to generate comprehensive dependency graphs, these have historically required significant processing time for each sentence or have traded accuracy for performance. In contrast, SedonaNLP currently employs a shallow dependency parsing method that runs in some cases 8-9X faster than earlier cited methods running on identical hardware. We choose a shallow approach with high, medium, and low confidence cutoffs after observing that roughly 80% of all captions con-

```
Caption 1 (Processing)
 1. A cat onthe floor watching a tv on a chair
           | |
 2. A cat on the floor watching a tv on a chair.

 3. A/DT cat/NN on/IN the/DT floor/NN watching/VBG a/DT tv/NN on/IN
    a/DT chair/NN ./.
 4. NX( A/DT cat/NN )      IX( on/IN )     NX( the/DT floor/NN )
    VX( watching/VBG )
    NX( a/DT tv/NN )      IX( on/IN )     NX( a/DT chair/NN )
5a. Subject    : NX( A/DT cat/NN ) IX( on/IN ) NX( the/DT floor/NN)
5b. Predicate: VX( watching/VBG )
5c. Object     : NX( a/DT tv/NN )  IX( on/IN ) NX( a/DT chair/NN )
5d. <A cat on the floor; watching; a tv on a chair>
 6. <cat; watching; tv>
 7. <cat; on; floor>
 8. <tv; on chair>

Extracted Facts

Caption 1| nVX01,nIN02 | <S;P;O> | ID NX IN NX VX=VBG NX IN NX
      <cat/NN on/IN floor/NN; watching/VBG; tv/NN on/IN chair/NN>
      <cat/NN; watching/VBG; tv/NN>
Caption 1| nVX01,nIN02 | <s;r;o>
      <cat; on; floor>
Caption 1| nVX01,nIN02 | <s;r;o>
      <tv; on; chair>
Caption 2| nVX01,nIN01 | <S;P;O> | ID NX IN NX VX=VBG NX
      <fat/JJ cat/NN in/IN living/JJ room/NN; watching/VBG; tv/NN>
      <cat/NN in/IN room/NN; watching/VBG; tv/NN>
      <cat/NN; watching/VBG; tv/NN>
Caption 2| nVX01,nIN01 | <S;A                >
      <cat; fat>
Caption 2| nVX01,nIN01 | <S;A                >
      <room; living>
Caption 2| nVX01,nIN01 | <s;r;o>
      <fat cat; in; living room>
```

Figure 4: Examples of caption processing and <S,P,O> and <S,P> structured fact extractions.

sisted of 0 or 1 Verb expressions (VX); see Fig. 3 for MSCOCO dataset (Lin et al., 2014). The top 500 image caption syntactic patterns we observed can be found on our supplemental materials (El-hoseiny et al., 2016b). These syntactic patterns are used to learn rules for automatic extraction for not only <S,P,O>, but also <S,P>, and <S,A>, where <S,P>, are subject-action facts and <S,A> are subject-attribute facts. Pattern examples and statistics for MS COCO are shown in Fig. 5.

In SedonaNLP, structured fact extraction was accomplished by learning a subset of abstract syntactic patterns consisting of basic noun, verb, and preposition expressions by analyzing 1.6M caption examples provided by the MS COCO, Flickr30K, and Stony Brook University Im2Text caption datasets. Our approach mirrors existing known art with the addition of internally-developed POS and clause tagging accuracy improvements through the use of heuristics listed

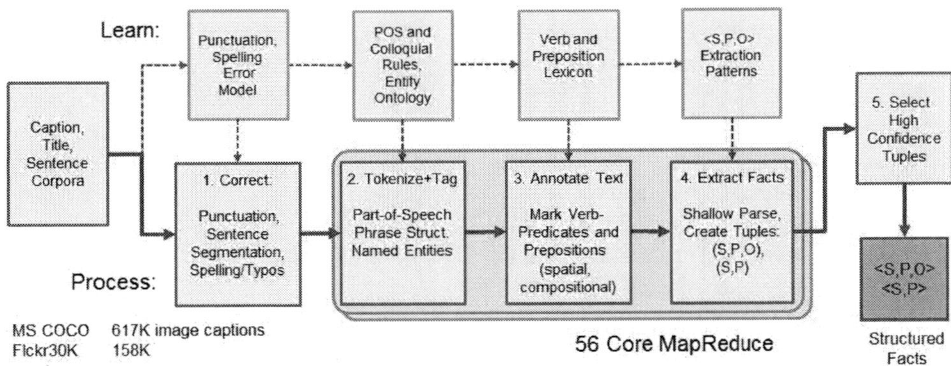

Figure 2: SedonaNLP Pipeline for Structured Fact Extraction from Captions

```
NX VX IN NX              #  1   10.19/10.19 NX(a blue street sign) VX(sitting) IN(under) NX(a camera)
NX VX IN NX IN NX        #  2    9.73/19.92 NX(a brown cat) VX(stares) IN(at) NX(something) IN(in) NX(the field)
NX VX NX IN NX           #  3    7.05/26.97 NX(some sheep) VX(eating) NX(grass) IN(in_front_of) NX(a rock)
NX IN NX IN NX           #  4    5.65/32.62 NX(a) IN(round) NX(blue street sign) IN(with) NX(a white arrow)
NX IN NX VX IN NX        #  5    3.27/35.89 NX(a sign) IN(in_front_of) NX(a fence) VX(laced) IN(with) NX(shrubbery)
NX IN NX                 #  6    3.00/38.89 NX(a orange cat) IN(with) NX(green eyes and long whiskers)
NX VX NX IN NX IN NX     #  7    1.77/40.67 NX(a) VX(very close) NX(shot) IN(of) NX(a cat's face) IN(in_front_of)
                                            NX(the camera)
NX IN NX IN NX IN NX     #  8    1.76/42.43 NX(a toddler reaches) IN(into) NX(a bowl) IN(of) NX(grapes) IN(in)
                                            NX(a sink)
NX IN NX CC NX           #  9    1.70/44.13 NX(a bathroom) IN(with) NX(two sinks mirrors) CC(and) NX(some bottles)
NX IN NX VX NX           # 10    1.69/45.82 NX(a person) IN(on) NX(a skate board) VX(does) NX(a trick)
```

Figure 5: Examples of the top observed Noun (NX), Verb (VX), and Preposition (IN) Syntactic patterns.

below to reduce higher occurrence errors due to systematic parsing errors: (i) Mapping past participles to adjectives (e.g., stained glass), (ii) De-nesting existential facts (e.g., this is a picture of a cat watching a tv.), (iii) Identifying auxiliary verbs (e.g., do verb forms).

In Fig. 4, we show an example of extracted <S,P,O> structured facts useful for image annotation for a small sample of MS COCO captions. Our initial experiments empirically confirmed the findings of IBM Watson PRISMATIC researchers who indicated big complex parse trees tend to have more wrong parses. By limiting a frame to be only a small subset of a complex parse tree, we reduce the chance of error parse in each frame (Fan et al., 2010). In practice, we observed many correctly extracted structured facts for the more complex sentences (i.e., sentences with multiple VX verb expressions and multiple spatial prepositional expressions) – these facts contained useful information that could have been used in our joint learning model but were conservatively filtered to help ensure the overall accuracy of the facts being presented to our system. As improvements are made to semantic triple extraction and confidence evaluation systems, we see potential in several areas to exploit more structured facts and to filter less information. Our full <S,P,O> triple and related

tuple extractions for MS COCO and Flickr30K datasets are available in the supplemental material (Elhoseiny et al., 2016b).

5 Locating facts in the Image

In this section, we present details about the second step of our automatic annotation process introduced in Sec. 3. After the candidate facts are extracted from the sentences, we end up with a set $\mathbf{F}_s = \{\mathbf{f}_l^i\}, i = 1 : N_s$ for statement s, where N_s is the number of extracted candidate fact $\mathbf{f}_l^i, \forall i$ from the statement s using either Clausie (Del Corro and Gemulla, 2013) or Sedona-3.0. The localization step is further divided into two steps. The mapping step maps nouns in the facts to candidate boxes in the image. The grounding step processes each fact associated with the candidate boxes and outputs a final bounding box if localization is successful. The two steps are detailed in the following subsections.

5.1 Mapping

The mapping step starts with a pre-processing step that filters out a non-useful subset of $\mathbf{F}_s$ and produces a more useful set $\mathbf{F}_s^*$ that we try to locate/ground in the image. We perform this step by performing word sense disambiguation using the state-of-the-art method (Zhong and Ng, 2010).

The word sense disambiguation method provides each word in the statement with a word sense in the wordNet ontology (Leacock and Chodorow, 1998). It also assigns for each word a part of speech tag. Hence, for each extracted candidate fact in $\mathbf{F}_s$ we can verify if it follows the expected part of speech according to (Zhong and Ng, 2010). For instance, all S should be nouns, all P should be either verbs or adjectives, and O should be nouns. This results in a filtered set of facts $\mathbf{F}_s^*$. Then, each S is associated with a set of candidate boxes in the image for second- and third-order facts and each O associated with a set or candidate boxes in the image for third-order facts only. Since entities in MSCOCO dataset and Flickr30K are annotated differently, we present how the candidate boxes are determined in each of these datasets.

MS COCO Mapping: Mapping to candidate boxes for MS COCO reduces to assigning the S for second-order and third-order facts, and S and O for third-order facts. Either S or O is assigned to one of the MSCOCO objects or SUN scenes classes. Given the word sense of the given part (S or O), we check if the given sense is a descendant of MSCOCO objects senses in the wordNet ontology. If it is, the given part (S or O) is associated with the set of candidate bounding boxes that belongs to the given object (e.g., all boxes that contain the "person" MSCOCO object is under the "person" wordnet node like "man", 'girl', etc). If the given part (S or O) is not an MSCOCO object or one of its descendants under wordNet, we further check if the given part is one of the SUN dataset scenes. If this condition holds, the given part is associated with a bounding box of the whole image.

Flickr30K Mapping: In contrast to MSCOCO dataset, the bounding box annotation comes for each entity in each statement in Flickr30K dataset. Hence, we compute the candidate bounding box annotations for each candidate fact by searching the entities in the same statement from which the clause is extracted. Candidate boxes are those that have the same name. Similarly, this process assigns S for second-order facts and assigns S and O for second- and third-order facts.

Having finished the mapping process, whether for MSCOCO or Flickr30K, each candidate fact $\mathbf{f}_l^i \in \mathbf{F}_s^*$, is associated with candidate boxes depending on its type as follows.

$<$**S,P**$>$: Each $\mathbf{f}_l^i \in \mathbf{F}_s^*$ of second-order type is associated with one set of bounding boxes $\mathbf{b}_S^i$,
which are the candidate boxes for the S part. $\mathbf{b}_O^i$ could be assumed to be always an empty set for second-order facts.

$<$**S,P,O**$>$: Each $\mathbf{f}_l^i \in \mathbf{F}_s^*$ of third-order type is associated with two sets of bounding boxes $\mathbf{b}_S^i$ and $\mathbf{b}_S^i$ as candidate boxes for the S and P parts, respectively.

5.2 Grounding

The grounding process is the process of associating each $\mathbf{f}_l^i \in \mathbf{F}_s^*$ with an image $\mathbf{f}_v$ by assigning f_l to a bounding box in the given MS COCO image scene given the $\mathbf{b}_S^i$ and $\mathbf{b}_O^i$ candidate boxes. The grounding process is relatively different for the two dataset due to the difference of the entity annotations.

Grounding: MS COCO dataset (Training and Validation sets)

In the MS COCO dataset, one challenging aspect is that the S or O can be singular, plural, or referring to the scene. This means that one S could map to multiple boxes in the image. For example, "people" maps to multiple boxes of "person". Furthermore, this case could exist for both the S and the O. In cases where either S or O is plural, the bounding box assigned is the union of all candidate bounding boxes in $\mathbf{b}_S^i$. The grounding then proceeds as follows.

$<$**S,P**$>$ **facts:**

(1) If the computed $\mathbf{b}_S^i = \varnothing$ for the given $\mathbf{f}_l^i$, then $\mathbf{f}_l^i$ fails to ground and is discarded.

(2) If S singular, $\mathbf{f}_v^i$ is the image region that with the largest candidate bounding box in $\mathbf{b}_S^i$.

(3) If S is plural, $\mathbf{f}_v^i$ is the image region that with union of the candidate bounding boxes in $\mathbf{b}_S^i$.

$<$**S,P, O**$>$ **facts:**

(1) If $\mathbf{b}_S^i = \varnothing$ and $\mathbf{b}_O^i = \varnothing$, $\mathbf{f}_l^i$ fails to ground and is ignored.

(2) If $\mathbf{b}_S^i \neq \varnothing$ and $\mathbf{b}_O^i \neq \varnothing$, then bounding boxes are assigned to S and O such that the distance between them is minimized (though if S or O is plural, the assigned bounding box is the union of all bounding boxes for $\mathbf{b}_S^i$ or $\mathbf{b}_O^i$ respectively), and the grounding is assigned the union of the bounding boxes assigned to S and O.

(3) If either $\mathbf{b}_S^i = \varnothing$ or $\mathbf{b}_O^i = \varnothing$, then a bounding box is assigned to the present object (the largest bounding box if singular, or the union of all bounding boxes if plural). If the area of this region compared to the area of the whole scene is greater than a threshold $th = 0.3$, then the $\mathbf{f}_v^i$ is associ-

Table 1: Human Subject Evaluation by MTurk workers %

Dataset (responses)	Q1		Q2		Q3						
	yes	no	Yes	No	a	b	c	d	e	f	g
MSCOCO train 2014 (4198)	89.06	10.94	87.86	12.14	64.58	12.64	3.51	5.10	0.86	1.57	11.73
MSCOCO val 2014 (3296)	91.73	8.27	91.01	8.99	66.11	14.81	3.64	4.92	1.00	0.70	8.83
Flickr30K Entities2015 (3296)	88.94	11.06	88.19	11.81	70.12	11.31	3.09	2.79	0.82	0.39	11.46
Total	89.84	10.16	88.93	11.07	66.74	12.90	3.42	4.34	0.89	0.95	10.76

Table 2: Human Subject Evaluation by Volunteers % (This is another set of annotations different from those evaluated by MTurkers)

Volunteers	Q1		Q2		Q3						
	yes	No	Yes	No	a	b	c	d	e	f	g
MSCOCO train 2014 (400)	90.75	9.25	91.25	8.75	73.5	8.25	2.75	6.75	0.5	0.5	7.75
MSCOCO val 2014 (90)	97.77	2.3	94.44	8.75	84.44	8.88	3.33	1.11	0	0	2.22
Flickr30K Entities 2015 (510)	78.24	21.76	73.73	26.27	64.00	4.3	1.7	1.7	0.7	1.18	26.45

ated to the whole image of the scene. Otherwise, $\mathbf{f}_l^i$ fails to ground and is ignored.

Grounding: Flickr30K dataset The main difference in Flickr30K is that for each entity phrase in a sentence, there is a box in the image. This means there is no need to have cases for single and plural. Since in this case, the word "men" in the sentence will be associated with the set of boxes referred to by "men" in the sentences. We union these boxes for plural words as one candidate box for "men"

We can also use the information that the object box has to refer to a word that is after the subject word, since subject usually occurs earlier in the sentence compared to object. We union these boxes for plural words.

<S,P> facts:

If the computed $\mathbf{b}_S^i = \varnothing$ for the given $\mathbf{f}_l^i$, then $\mathbf{f}_l^i$ fails to ground and is discarded. Otherwise, the fact is assigned to the largest candidate box in if there are multiple boxes.

<S,P, O> facts: <S,P, O> facts are handled very similar to MSCOCO dataset with two main differences.

a) The candidate boxes are computed as described for the case of Flickr30K dataset.

b) All cases are handled as single case, since even plural words are assigned one box based on the nature of the annotations in this dataset.

6 Experiments

6.1 Human Subject Evaluation

We propose three questions to evaluate each annotation: (Q1) Is the extracted fact correct (Yes/No)? The purpose of this question is to evaluate errors captured by the first step, which extracts facts by Sedona or Clausie. (Q2) Is the fact located in the image (Yes/No)? In some cases, there might be a fact mentioned in the caption that does not exist in the image and is mistakenly considered as an annotation. (Q3) How accurate is the box assigned to a given fact (a to g)? a (about right), b (a bit big), c (a bit small), d (too small), e (too big), f (totally wrong box), g (fact does not exist or other). Our instructions on these questions to the participants can be found in this url (Eval, 2016).

We evaluate these three questions for the facts that were successfully assigned a box in the image, because the main purpose of this evaluation is to measure the usability of the collected annotations as training data for our model. We created an Amazon Mechanical Turk form to ask these three questions. So far, we collected a total of 10,786 evaluation responses, which are an evaluation of 3,595 ($\mathbf{f}_v$, $\mathbf{f}_l$) pairs (3 responses/ pair). Table 2 shows the evaluation results, which indicate that the data is useful for training, since≈83.1% of them are correct facts with boxes that are either about right, or a bit big or small (a,b,c). We further some evaluation responses that we collected from volunteer researchers in Table 2 showing similar results.

Fig. 6 shows some successful qualitative results that include four extracted structured facts from MS COCO dataset (e.g., <person, using, phone>, <person, standing>, etc). Fig 7 also show a negative example where there is a wrong fact among the extracted facts (i.e., <house, ski>). The main reason for this failure case is that "how" is mistyped as "house"; see Fig 7. The supplementary materials (Elhoseiny et al., 2016b) includes all the captions of these examples and also additional qualitative examples.

6.2 Hardness Evaluation of the collected data

In order to study how the method behave in both easy and hard examples. This section present statistics of the successfully extracted facts and relate it to the hardness of the extraction of these facts. We start by defining hardness of an extracted fact in our case and its dependency on the fact type. Our method collect both second- and third-order facts. We refer to candidate subjects as all instances of the entity in the image that match the subject type of either a second-order fact <S,P> or a third-order fact <S,P,O>. We refer to candidate objects as all instances in the image that match the object type of a third-order fact <S,P,O>. The selection of the candidate subjects and candidate objects is a part of our method that we detailed in Sec 5. We define the hardness for second order facts by the number of candidate subjects and the hardness of third order facts by the number of candidate subjects multiplied by the number of candidate objects.

In Fig 8 and 9, the Y axis is the number of facts for each bin. The X axis shows the bins that correspond to hardness that we defined for both second and third order fats. Figure 8 shows a histogram of the difficulties for all Mturk evaluated examples including both the successful and the failure cases. Figure 9 shows a similar histogram but for but for subset of facts verified by the Turkers with Q3 as (about right). The figures show that the method is able to handle difficulty cases even with more than 150 possibilities for grounding. We show these results broken out for MSCOCO and Flickr30K Entities datasets and for each fact types in the supplementary materials (Elhoseiny et al., 2016b).

Figure 6: Several Facts successfully extracted by our method from two MS COCO scenes

Figure 7: An example where one of the extracted facts are not correct due to a spelling mistake

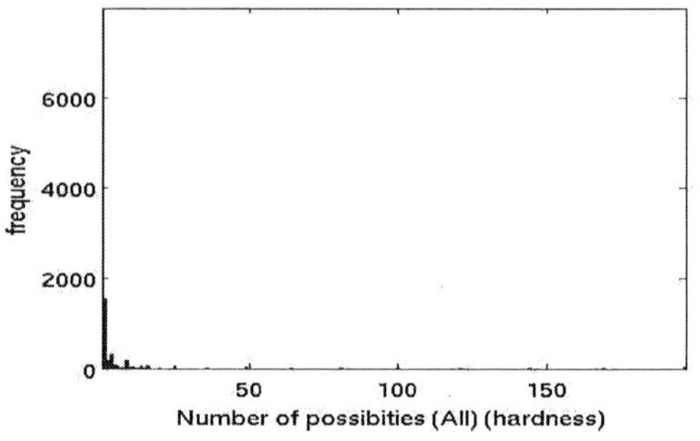

Figure 8: (All MTurk Data) Hardness histogram after candidate box selection using our method

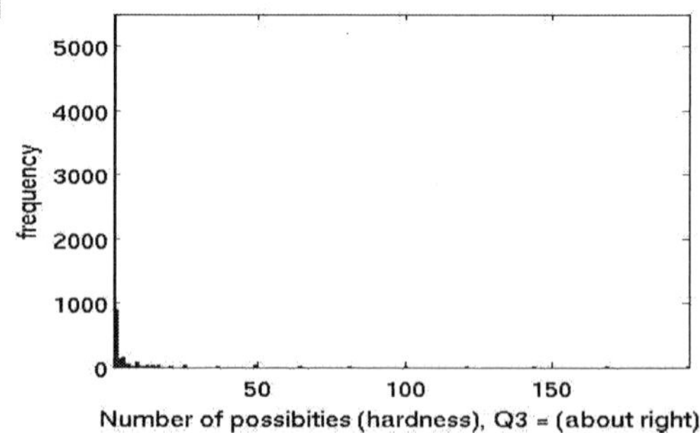

Figure 9: (MTurk Data with Q3=about right)Hardness histogram after our candidate box selection

7 Conclusion

We present a new method whose main purpose to collect visual fact annotation by a language approach. The collected data help train visual system systems on the fact level with the diversity of facts captured by any fact described by an image caption. We showed the effectiveness of the proposed methodology by extracting hundreds of thousands of fact-level annotations from

MSCOCO and Flickr30K datasets. We verified and analyzed the collected data and showed that more than 80% of the collected data are good for training visual systems.

References

Stanislaw Antol, Aishwarya Agrawal, Jiasen Lu, Margaret Mitchell, Dhruv Batra, C Lawrence Zitnick, and Devi Parikh. 2015. Vqa: Visual question answering. In *ICCV*.

Jason Baldridge. 2014. The opennlp project. *URL: http://opennlp.apache.org/index.html,(accessed 2 February 2014)*.

Xinlei Chen, Ashish Shrivastava, and Arpan Gupta. 2013. Neil: Extracting visual knowledge from web data. In *ICCV*.

Jinho D Choi. 2014. Clearnlp.

Luciano Del Corro and Rainer Gemulla. 2013. Clausie: clause-based open information extraction. In *WWW*.

Santosh K Divvala, Alireza Farhadi, and Carlos Guestrin. 2014. Learning everything about anything: Webly-supervised visual concept learning. In *CVPR*.

Mohamed Elhoseiny, Scott Cohen, Walter Chang, Brian Price, and Ahmed Elgammal. 2016a. Sherlock: Scalable fact learning in images.

Mohamed Elhoseiny, Scott Cohen, Walter Cheng, Brian Price, and Ahmed Elgammal. 2016b. Autoomatic annotation of structured facts in images- supplementary materials. `https://www.dropbox.com/s/22m6jxvtqhhg10q/supplementary.zip?dl=0`. [Online; accessed 19-Nov-2015].

SAFA Eval. 2016. Safa eval instructions. `https://dl.dropboxusercontent.com/u/479679457/Sherlock_SAFA_eval_Instructions.html`. [Online; accessed 02-March-2016].

James Fan, David Ferrucci, David Gondek, and Aditya Kalyanpur. 2010. Prismatic: Inducing knowledge from a large scale lexicalized relation resource. In *NAACL HLT*. Association for Computational Linguistics.

Andrej Karpathy, Armand Joulin, and Fei Fei F Li. 2014. Deep fragment embeddings for bidirectional image sentence mapping. In *Advances in neural information processing systems*, pages 1889–1897.

Ryan Kiros, Ruslan Salakhutdinov, and Richard S Zemel. 2015. Unifying visual-semantic embeddings with multimodal neural language models. *TACL*.

Claudia Leacock and Martin Chodorow. 1998. Combining local context and wordnet similarity for word sense identification. *WordNet: An electronic lexical database*.

Tsung-Yi Lin, Michael Maire, Serge Belongie, James Hays, Pietro Perona, Deva Ramanan, Piotr Dollár, and C Lawrence Zitnick. 2014. Microsoft coco: Common objects in context. In *ECCV*. Springer.

Mateusz Malinowski, Marcus Rohrbach, and Mario Fritz. 2015. Ask your neurons: A neural-based approach to answering questions about images. In *ICCV*.

Christopher D Manning, Mihai Surdeanu, John Bauer, Jenny Finkel, Steven J Bethard, and David Mc-Closky. 2014. The stanford corenlp natural language processing toolkit. In *Proceedings of 52nd Annual Meeting of the Association for Computational Linguistics: System Demonstrations*, pages 55–60.

Junhua Mao, Wei Xu, Yi Yang, Jiang Wang, and Alan Yuille. 2015. Deep captioning with multimodal recurrent neural networks (m-rnn). *ICLR*.

George A Miller. 1995. Wordnet: a lexical database for english. *Communications of the ACM*.

Bryan Plummer, Liwei Wang, Chris Cervantes, Juan Caicedo, Julia Hockenmaier, and Svetlana Lazebnik. 2015. Flickr30k entities: Collecting region-to-phrase correspondences for richer image-to-sentence models. In *ICCV*.

Mengye Ren, Ryan Kiros, and Richard Zemel. 2015. Exploring models and data for image question answering. In *NIPS*.

Delia Rusu, Lorand Dali, Blaz Fortuna, Marko Grobelnik, and Dunja Mladenic. 2007. Triplet extraction from sentences. In *International Multiconference" Information Society-IS*.

Oriol Vinyals, Alexander Toshev, Samy Bengio, and Dumitru Erhan. 2015. Show and tell: A neural image caption generator.

Jianxiong Xiao, James Hays, Krista Ehinger, Aude Oliva, Antonio Torralba, et al. 2010. Sun database: Large-scale scene recognition from abbey to zoo. In *CVPR*.

Kelvin Xu, Jimmy Ba, Ryan Kiros, Aaron Courville, Ruslan Salakhutdinov, Richard Zemel, and Yoshua Bengio. 2015. Show, attend and tell: Neural image caption generation with visual attention. In *ICML*.

Zhi Zhong and Hwee Tou Ng. 2010. It makes sense: A wide-coverage word sense disambiguation system for free text. In *ACL*.

Combining Lexical and Spatial Knowledge to Predict Spatial Relations between Objects in Images

Manuela Hürlimann
The Insight Centre for Data Analytics
National University of Ireland Galway
IDA Business Park, Lower Dangan, Galway
manuela.huerlimann@insight-centre.org

Johan Bos
Center for Language and Cognition
University of Groningen
The Netherlands
johan.bos@rug.nl

Abstract

Explicit representations of images are useful for linguistic applications related to images. We design a representation based on first-order models that capture the objects present in an image as well as their spatial relations. We take a supervised learning approach to the spatial relation classification problem and study the effects of spatial and lexical information on prediction performance. We find that lexical information is required to accurately predict spatial relations when combined with location information, achieving an F-score of 0.80, compared to a most-frequent-class baseline of 0.62.

1 Introduction

In the light of growing amount of digital image data, methods for automatically linking data to language are a great asset. Due to recent advances in the distinct areas of language technology and computer vision, research combining the two fields has become increasingly popular, including automatical generation of captions (Karpathy and Fei-Fei, 2014, Elliott and Keller, 2013, Elliott et al., 2014, Kulkarni et al., 2011, Vinyals et al., 2014, Yang et al., 2011) and translation of text into visual scenes (Coyne et al., 2010).

One task which has not yet been extensively researched is the automatic derivation of rich abstract representations from images (Neumann and Möller, 2008, Malinowski and Fritz, 2014). A formal representation of an image goes beyond naming the objects that are present; it can also account for some of the *structure* of the visual scene by including spatial relations between objects. This information could enhance the interface between language and vision. Imagine, for instance, searching for images that show a "man riding a bicycle": it is necessary, but not sufficient, for pictures to contain both a man and a bicycle. In order to satisfy the query, the man also has to be somehow connected to the bicycle, with his feet on the pedals and his hands on the steering bar.

We argue that representations of images which take into account spatial relations can enable more sophisticated interactions between language and vision that go beyond basic object co-occurrence. The aim of this paper is to use an extension of first-order models to represent images of real situations. In order to obtain such models, we need (a) high-quality, broad-coverage object localisation and identification and methods to (b) accurately determine object characteristics and to (c) detect spatial relationships between objects.

As broad-coverage object detection systems are not yet available, we carry out steps (a) and (b) manually. Hence, in this paper, we focus on step (c): the detection of spatial relations. This is difficult because there is a vast number of ways in which a given relation can be realised in a visual scene. The questions that we want to answer are whether first-order models of classical logic are appropriate to represent images, and what features are suitable for detecting spatial relationships between objects in images. In particular, we want to investigate what the impact of lexical knowledge is on determining spatial relations, independent of the quality of object recognition.

This paper is organised as follows. We will first give more background about spatial relations (Section 2) and related work on combining vision with language technology (Section 3). Then we will introduce our data set in Section 4, comprising a hundred images with a total of 583 located objects for which spatial relations need to be determined. In Section 5 we outline our classification method in detail and present and discuss our results.

Proceedings of the 5th Workshop on Vision and Language, pages 10–18,
Berlin, Germany, August 12 2016. ©2016 Association for Computational Linguistics

2 Background: Spatial Relations

In this paper we focus on the task of predicting spatial relations in images, investigating three relations (part-of, touching, supports; see Section 4). We integrate the detected spatial relations into first-order models borrowed from logic, which offer an easily extendable representation of an image. Once detected, spatial relations can also serve as a useful basis for predicting more specific predicates which hold between objects, such as actions. For example, "ride" presupposes touching, and "carry" or "hold" presuppose that the object being carried or held is supported by the other object. The spatial configuration of two objects restricts the spatial relations which are possible (and plausible) between them; for example, two objects can only touch if they are in sufficient proximity to each other. Knowledge of objects properties further constrains the set of plausible relations. For example, if asked to determine whether the two objects in Figure 1 are in a part-of relationship, the decision is difficult on spatial grounds alone, that is, not knowing *what* objects are (indicated by blackening the picture). In this case, the spatial configuration on its own does not supply sufficient information to confidently answer this question.

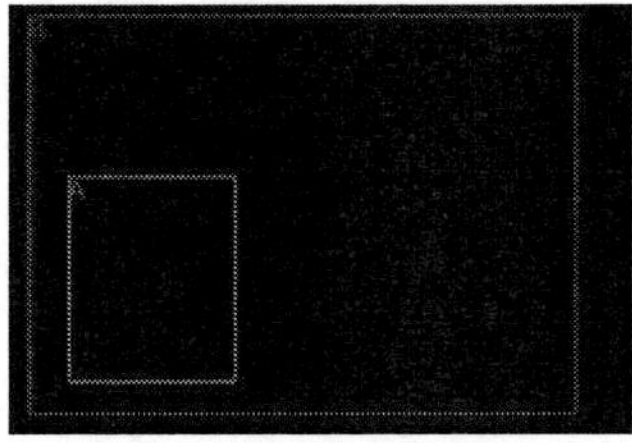

Figure 1: Is A (red) part of B (blue)? We can't tell: we need semantic knowledge of A and B.

However, information about the objects themselves, beyond their locations, improves spatial relation prediction. Consider Figure 2: when we reveal the object identities, we can be very certain that the ice cream and boy are *not* in a part-of relationship, but the cat and head are. Such inferences about spatial relations are straightforward for humans, while this is a difficult task for computers. We suggest, however, that useful machine-readable world knowledge can be gleaned from lexical resources such as WordNet (Miller, 1995) and large text corpora.

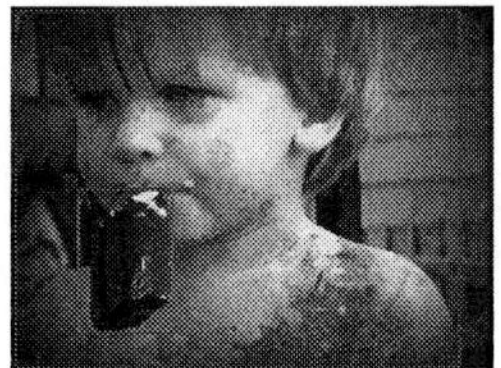

Figure 2: A *not* part of B (left); A part of B (right)

While many researchers have focused on generating textual descriptions for images (Karpathy and Fei-Fei, 2014, Elliott and Keller, 2013, Elliott et al., 2014, Kulkarni et al., 2011, Vinyals et al., 2014, Yang et al., 2011), deriving a first-order semantic model from an image is a task hitherto unattempted. The advantage of having an abstract model instead of a textual label is the ease with which *inferences* can be made. Inference processes include querying the model and checking for consistency and informativeness. This greatly facilitates maintenance of image databases and enables applications such as question answering and image retrieval (Elliott et al., 2014).

3 Related Work

Research into combining Natural Language Processing and Computer Vision has become increasingly popular over the past years. There is an extensive body of work, among others in the following areas: building multimodal models of meaning which take into account both text and image data (Bruni et al., 2012), generating images from textual data (Lazaridou et al., 2015, Coyne et al., 2010), Question Answering on images (Malinowski and Fritz, 2014), and automatic image label generation (Karpathy and Fei-Fei, 2014, Elliott and Keller, 2013, Elliott et al., 2014, Kulkarni et al., 2011, Vinyals et al., 2014, Yang et al., 2011).

Belz et al. (2015) present a method for selecting prepositions to describe spatial relationships between objects in images. They use features based on geometrical configurations of bounding boxes as well as prior probabilities of prepositions occurring with objects/class labels.

Several approaches have been proposed to reason on spatial information derived from visual input. Neumann and Möller (2008) discuss the potential of knowledge representation for high-level scene interpretation. Their focus is on Description Logic (DL), a subset of first-order predicate calculus supporting inferences about various aspects of the scene. They identify requirements and processes for a system conducting stepwise inferences about concepts in a scene. This would make use of low-level visual and contextual information, spatial constraints, as well as taxonomic and compositional links between objects. As their work is a conceptual exploration of the area, they do not specify how they would acquire such a knowledge base with information about object relations and contexts.

Falomir et al. (2011) aim at creating a qualitative description of a scene (image or video still) and translating it into Description Logic. Object characteristics of interest include shape and colour as well as spatial relations. The latter are based on topology and include *disjoint*, *touching*, *completely inside*, and *container* as well as information about relative orientation of objects. All qualitative descriptions are aggregated into an ontology with a shared vocabulary, which aids the inference of new knowledge using reasoning.

Zhu et al. (2014) present a Knowledge Base (KB) approach to predicting affordances (possibilities of interacting with objects - e.g. the handle on a teacup is an affordance for holding). Evidence in their Markov Logic Network KB consists of: affordances (actions), human poses, five relative spatial locations of objects with respect to the human (*above*, *in-hand*, *on-top*, *below*, *next-to*), and the following kinds of attributes: visual (material, shape, etc; obtained using a visual attribute classifier), physical (weight, size; obtained from online shopping sites), and categorical (hypernym information from WordNet). They stress the importance of inference, which is an essential benefit of their approach. Their results for zero-shot affordance prediction show a clear improvement compared to classifier-based approaches, underlining the strength of the KB approach. They find that categorical ("lexical") attributes boost performance.

4   The Image Model Collection

Below we present GrImSem-100 (Groningen Image Semantics - 100), the dataset used in the present work, which comprises a set of images paired with image models. The image models contain the first-order objects present in the images together with their spatial relations. First we describe the selected images and how we annotated them with spatial relations. Then we show what kind of models we use to represent the images.

4.1   Selected Images

Our dataset consists of one hundred images with associated first-order semantic models. We carefully hand-picked copyright-free images from an existing large image resource.[1] The selected images are shown in Figure 3. In the image selection

Figure 3: Selected images of our corpus.

process only images were chosen that contained two or more clearly visible concrete real-world objects, in order to get image material interesting for investigating spatial relation between various objects. As a result, typical images are of dogs chasing cats, human beings or animals eating something, or people riding their bicycle.

Selection of objects to annotate was mostly based on object size (large objects are annotated, small ones omitted), but exceptions were made for small objects which were striking or interesting. Each object was captured by a *bounding box*, also known as a "Minimal Bounding Rectangle" (MBR), a often used approximation to identify object in images (Wang, 2003). The bounding box of an object (Figure 4) is simply a rectangle covering all of its extent, thus preserving the object's "position and extension" (Wang, 2003). In total, 583 objects from 139 different synset categories were annotated across the 100 images.

4.2   Spatial Relations

In the scope of this paper we investigated three spatial relations:

- `part-of`

[1]Pixabay, `https://pixabay.com/en/`. All images are free to use, modify and distribute under the Creative Commons Public Domain Deed CC0 `https://creativecommons.org/publicdomain/zero/1.0/`, for both commercial and academic purposes

Figure 4: Bounding boxes with coordinates.

- `touching`
- `supports`

We selected `part of`, `touching` and `supports` for prediction because they are well-defined and less fuzzy than for example "far" or "near" / "close". `Part of` is closely connected to the part meronymy relation from lexical semantics and therefore interesting for our approach, which uses lexical knowledge. `Touches` and `supports` can be considered useful for predicting further predicates, such as actions. Additionally, we annotated a fourth spatial relation in the models, `occludes`, because we thought it would be an important feature in predicting the other three spatial relations. Below we discuss the properties of each of these relations.

Part-of If object A is `part-of` object B, then A and B form an entity such that if we removed A, B would not be the same entity any more and could not function in the usual way (e.g. A - wheel, B - bicycle). The `part-of` relation is transitive and asymmetric. Furthermore, no object can be `part-of` itself.

Touching Two objects A and B are `touching` if they have at least one point in common; they are not disjoint. Only solid and fluid, but not gaseous objects (such as "sky") can be in a `touching` relation. `Touching` is always symmetric but not necessarily transitive.

Supports In order for object A to `support` object B, the two objects need to be `touching`. `Support` means that the position of A depends on B: if B was not there, A would be in a different position. Therefore, there is the notion of "support against gravity", discussed by Sjöö et al. (2012, p.8). `Supports` can be mutual (symmet-

ric), but this is not a requirement; in fact, asymmetric support is probably more frequent. Furthermore, `supports` is transitive. For example, if a table supports a plate, and the plate supports a piece of cake, then the table also supports the piece of cake.

Occludes If object A `occludes` object B, it renders it partly invisible. Occlusion is viewpoint-sensitive: from the point of view of the observer, object A is partly in front of object B. For example, in Figure 6, the cat occludes the armchair.

4.3 Annotating Spatial Relations

We used the Crowdflower crowdsourcing platform to annotate the gold standard for the three spatial relations. In all annotation tasks, workers were presented with an image which had two objects highlighted in bounding boxes (one red and one blue). They had to choose the statement which they deemed to best describe the relationship between the two objects. To facilitate identification of objects in cluttered pictures, we provided the first WordNet lemma of the synset as a label for each box, prefixing with "A" and "B" for the directed relations `part-of` and `supports`. Figure 5 shows an example question as presented in the `part-of` task.

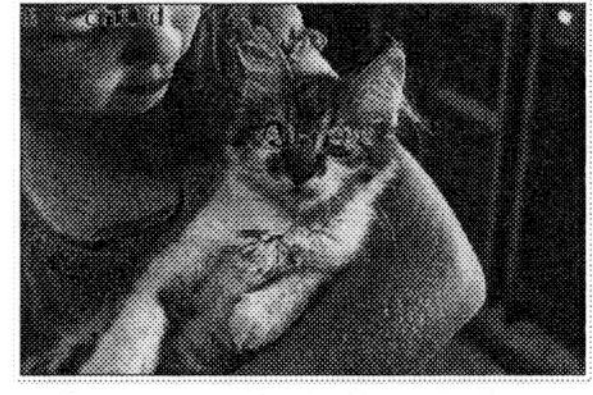

Figure 5: Example question presented to Crowdflower workers on `part-of` task.

Post-processing of the raw annotation results was done using the Multi-Annotator Confidence Estimation tool, MACE (Hovy et al., 2013). MACE is designed to evaluate data from categorical multi-annotator tasks. It provides competence ratings for individual annotators as well as the most probable answer for each item. A subsample of the MACE output was assessed manually and errors found during this inspection were corrected. However, a little bit of noise is likely to remain in the final spatial relation annotations.

4.4 Image Models and Grounding

In classical logic, a first-order model $M = \langle D, F \rangle$ has two components, a non-empty *domain* D (also called *universe*) and an *interpretation function* F (Blackburn and Bos, 2005). The domain is the set of all entities occurring in the model, and the interpretation function maps non-logical symbols from the vocabulary to these entities. We adopt the Prolog-readable model format of Blackburn & Bos for for our set of 100 images.

Each image is thus paired with a model that describes its key features, providing a simplified representation of the reality depicted in the image. The *vocabulary* of non-logical symbols present in the models is based on WordNet (Miller, 1995): we use the names of noun *synsets* as one-place predicates to name entities, and those of adjectives for modelling attributes (such as colours). Hyperonyms from a pruned top-level ontology were also semi-automatically added to the model to further enrich the image models. Additionally, we introduce two-place relations for the four spatial relations introduced in the previous section: s_part_of, s_touch, s_supports, and s_occludes.

Since we also model spatial characteristics of the situations at hand, we need to be able to ground the entities in the model to its physical location in the image. We do this with the help of a *grounding* function G. As a consequence, our grounded first-order models are defined as $M = \langle D, F, G \rangle$. The grounding function maps the domain entities to their coordinates, that is, the location in pixel space represented by bounding boxes. For the coordinates, we use the Pascal VOC notation (Everingham and Winn, 2012, p. 13), as illustrated in Figure 4. All distances are measured in pixels. An example of a model including Domain D, Interpretation Function F and Grounding G can be seen in Figure 6.

5 Predicting Spatial Relations

5.1 Instances

Based on our image-model dataset (see Section 4), we create a set of object pairs for classification purposes. All ordered combinations of two objects (pairs) within an image are considered, giving us a total of 1,515 instances for classification. We randomly split the instances (across all images), using 90% (1,364 pairs) for training purposes and reserving 10% (151 pairs) as unseen test data.

Figure 6: Image and grounded first-order model.

Table 1: Distribution of class labels in training and testing data.

relation	train	test	overall
A part of B	16	2	18
B part of A	148	16	164
A and B touch	137	16	153
A and B touch + A supp B	86	9	95
A and B touch + B supp A	119	14	133
no relation	858	94	952
total	1,364	151	1,515

5.2 Task Formulations

We cast the spatial relation prediction task as a classification problem, in which each instance belongs to one of the following disjoint classes:

- A part of B
- B part of A
- A and B touch
- A and B touch + A supports B
- A and B touch + B supports A
- no relation: A and B are in no relation

Table 1 shows the distribution of the classes across the training and testing (unseen) data.

We distinguish two subtasks according to the set of instances selected for classification:

- **Subtask A:** predicting relation existence and types (all instances)
- **Subtask B:** predicting relation types only (excluding the class "no relation")

We use a multi-label formulation, i.e. the labels *A part of B*, *B part of A*, *touching*, *A supports B* and *B supports A* are used, and each instance can have multiple labels (or none).

5.3 Features

5.3.1 Spatial Features

The spatial features capture knowledge about the spatial properties of (pairs of) objects.

Overlap   This consists of two features:

- a boolean: do the two bounding boxes have at least one pixel in common?
- the size of this overlap, that is, the number of pixels that the two bounding boxes share

Contained-in   Two booleans expressing whether (i) the bounding box of the first object is entirely contained within that of the second object or (ii) vice versa.

Object size   We approximate true size by using the surface area of the corresponding bounding box (in pixels). In order to account for the effects of object truncation, varying image sizes and perspectives, we average in two steps for each synset. First, we normalise the size (width x height) of each object in each image by the width and height of the image.   Second, we average these normalised surface areas for each object type (e.g. `cat.n.01`) across all images, obtaining the following features:

- The size of the first object
- The size of the second object
- The absolute difference in size between the first and the second object

Occlusion   Occlusion carries information about the depth alignment of objects. An object occludes another if it partially renders it invisible (see Section 4.2). CrowdFlower was used to annotate occlusion (see Section 4.3).

5.3.2 Lexical Features

Lexical features capture linguistics knowledge about objects from WordNet and corpora.

Meronymy (part-whole relation)   For a pair of objects (A, B) we determine whether A is a part meronym of B, or B is a part meronym of A (two boolean features).

Hypernymy   In addition to information about meronyny (`has-a`), we also consider the ontological `is-a` status of objects.   We use a top-level pruned ontology, which is divided into ten levels, to obtain the following features for each level (Blanchard et al., 2005):

1. Are the hypernyms identical? (boolean)
2. Path similarity of the hypernyms (range 0-1)
3. Leacock-Chodorow (LCH) similarity (no fixed range)
4. Wu-Palmer (WUP) similarity (no fixed range)

Corpus features   Useful information about objects can be gleaned from large text collections. We thus use co-occurrence data from the first ten subcorpora of the ukWaC corpus comprising 92.5 million words (Baroni et al., 2009).

For each instance, we extract all uni-, bi- and trigrams (excluding sentence-final punctuation) that occur between lemmas of the first and lemmas of the second object. From these data, we extract the following feature sub-groups:

1. prepositions (pos-tag `IN`) - e.g. "cat *on* (the) lawn"
2. verb forms of "to have" and "to be" (pos-tags `VH.?` and `VB.?`)
3. verb forms of other verbs (pos-tag `VV.?`)

We consider single prepositions and verbs as well as sequences of two prepositions or two verbs. The raw data for prepositions and "other" verbs are reduced according to greatest coverage, retaining 50 and 100, respectively. In classification, for an ordered pair of objects, we use the *frequency* with which the given verb or preposition occurs across all lemma pairs as a feature.

Word embeddings   Word embeddings are another way to make use of co-occurrence data. We use the pre-trained 300-dimensional `word2vec` vectors by Mikolov et al. (2013a) and Mikolov et al. (2013b). These vectors were trained on a 100 billion-word subpart of the Google News dataset. We calculate the vector for each synset as an average across the vectors of all its lemmas. In order to obtain features from a pair of synsets the second vector is subtracted from the first and each dimension of the resulting vector is added as a feature (300 features).

5.4 Results

We evaluate prediction performance using the F1-score, obtained using 5-fold stratified cross-validation and averaged across two runs. We report scores for each relation as well as micro-averaged overall scores.

Combo1	configuration — bounding box overlap, contained in, occlusion (6 features)
Combo2	size (3 features)
Combo3	meronymy (2 features)
Combo4	hypernym identity (10 features)
Combo5	hypernym similarity measures (30 features)
Combo6	co-occurrence frequency with prepositions (50 features)
Combo7	word embedding subtraction (300 features)
Combo8	co-occurrence frequency with verbs other than "to have" and "to be" (100 features)
Combo9	co-occurrence frequency with "to have" and "to be" (7 features)

Table 2: Feature combinations.

	subtask A	subtask B
baseline	0.62	0.41
single groups	0.71[a]	0.74[b]
only spatial (groups 1 + 2)	0.78	0.82
only lexical (groups 3-9)	0.68	0.72
best lexical+spatial	**0.80**[c]	**0.85**[d]

[a] Group 3 (meronymy), best single group in subtask A
[b] Group 1 (spatial configuration), best single group in subtask B
[c] 1+2+3+5, best combination in subtask A
[d] 1+2+3+9, best combination in subtask B

Table 3: Summary of results on training data (overall F-scores).

	subtask A	subtask B
baseline	0.62	0.41
single groups	0.65	0.72
only spatial (groups 1 + 2)	0.80	0.80
only lexical (groups 3-9)	0.66	0.69
best lexical+spatial	**0.82**	**0.86**

Table 4: Summary of results on unseen test data (overall F-scores).

A baseline choosing the most frequent label(s) would assign "no relation" in subtask A (achieving 0.623), and `touching` (without an additional `supports` label) in subtask B (achieving 0.405).

Another point of comparison is the work by Rosman and Ramamoorthy (2011). They use a data-driven contact-point approach to classify 132 instances into three different relations. They achieve an overall F-score of 0.72, with results for individual relations ranging between 0.47 to 0.84.[2]

In order to assess the effect of the spatial and lexical features, we divide the features up into the groups shown in Table 2 (Combo1 and Combo2 are spatial features, while Combo3-9 are lexical features).

We test all possible combinations without replacement of the nine groups in the range 1 to 9, separately on (i) the set of all instances (subtask A) and on (ii) the set of instances which are in a relation (subtask B). In order to evaluate the results, we calculate the average F-score for each single feature group (1, 2, 3, ...) as well as for combinations of feature groups (1+2, 1+2+3, 1+2+3+4, ...). There are 511 possible combinations.

In Table 3 we report the baselines, the best single groups (Combo3 (meronymy) in subtask A; Combo1 (spatial configuration in subtask B), spatial groups only, lexical groups only and the best respective combinations per subtask (1+2+3+5 in subtask A; 1+2+3+9 in subtask B). A number of interesting things can be observed: first, all approaches significantly outperform the baselines if we combine multiple groups of features. Second,

performance on subtask B is generally better than on subtask A, indicating that pre-selecting object pairs which are in a relation facilitates prediction. Third, the combined spatial feature groups perform better than the combined lexical feature groups; however, the best models are those which *combine* features from the spatial and lexical domain. Experiments on the reserved test set (see Table 4) further confirm that overfitting is not an issue and that the results obtained using cross-validation are robust.

Looking at performance for the individual relations, we find that `part-of` yields the best results[3] (achieving F-scores of 0.95 in subtask A and 0.96 in subtask B), while `touching` is the most difficult to predict (0.48 in subtask A - below baseline; 0.76 in subtask B). For `supports` we achieve 0.71 on subtask A and 0.88 on subtask B, and no relation (only in subtask A) scores 0.88.

5.5 Error Analysis

Tables 5 and 6 show the confusion matrices for the respective best-performing combinations of feature groups. Generally, it is straightforward to identify the direction of a relation, that is, to distinguish between A part of B and

---

[2] These figures were calculated from the confusion matrix in Rosman and Ramamoorthy (2011, p. 16).

[3] F-scores mentioned are from classification optimised for individual relations.

true \ assigned	A part of B	B part of A	touching	A supports B	B supports A	no relation
A part of B	**13**	0	0	0	0	3
B part of A	10	**139**	4	0	0	5
touching	10	6	**73**	1	5	52
A supports B	10	0	22	**43**	1	20
B supports A	10	0	21	1	**66**	31
no relation	10	3	67	6	17	**765**

Table 5: Confusion matrix for subtask A, using feature groups 1, 2, 3 and 5.

true \ assigned	A part of B	B part of A	touching	A supports B	B supports A	no relation
A part of B	**14**	0	2	0	0	0
B part of A	1	**143**	4	0	0	1
touching	1	8	**114**	3	10	2
A supports B	1	0	17	**65**	3	1
B supports A	1	0	26	2	**91**	0

Table 6: Confusion matrix for subtask B, using feature groups 1, 2, 3 and 9.

`B part of A` and between `A supports B` and `B supports A`. We can see from Table 5 that instances which are in "no relation" (the majority class) can be identified rather unambiguously, and also the distinction between `part-of` versus `touching` / `supports` can be easily made. However, there is considerable confusion between `touching` and `support`, which are fairly frequently confused for each other, as well as for "no relation", if present. The distinction between `touching` and "no relation" is presumably due to the incidental nature of the former (`touching` strongly dependets on the local spatial configurations, but can be ambiguous / difficult to see). Pixel-level features could help improve discrimination for these. `touching` and `supports` are difficult to distinguish because they are very similar. Since `supports` is misclassified as `touching` much more often than vice versa, more discriminative features for the former need to be found in order to resolve this issue. These could address object properties such as mass/weight, but also a refinement of the prepositional features already implemented could help, for example association measures such as Mutual Information instead of the simple co-occurrence

frequencies used in the present system.

6 Conclusions and Future Work

First-order models, as used in classical logic, are suitable for representing images in an abstract way. The entities in a model can be mapped to non-logical symbols from an existing ontology (we used WordNet in this paper). Spatial relations between entities can be simply added to the models. The models can be simply extended with a function that maps entities to the coordinates of the bounding boxes in images.

We developed a corpus of images depicting real situations with their first-order models, effectively linking visual scenes to language. Some of the aspects involved in this process were carried out manually, such as recognizing objects in an image, but it is not unthinkable that in the future software components could fulfil this task. We trained a classifier for recognising spatial relations between objects, and what we learn is that linguistic information is required to accurately predict these relations when combined with location information. The best performance (F-scores of 0.81 and 0.85 for subtasks A and B, respectively) was obtained when combining spatial and lexical feature groups, significantly outperforming either spatial or lexical features on their own.

The corpus of images paired with spatial models that arose from this work could be used for various research topics in the future. Currently the corpus is being extended to include more images and more spatial relations. One of the relations that we are currently investigating is the vague spatial relation `near`. The corpus also contains human-generated false and true descriptions with respect to the images. In the future we want to find out whether image models as proposed in this paper are helpful to verify the truth of a statement with respect to an image.

Acknowledgments

The first author was supported by the Erasmus Mundus Programme in Language and Communication Technologies (EM LCT) and partly by the SSIX Horizon 2020 project (grant agreement No 645425) and Science Foundation Ireland (SFI) under Grant Number SFI/12/RC/2289. Thanks to the Computational Semantics class in Groningen for supplying the initial models. We would like to thank Benno Weck and the anonymous reviewers for their helpful comments.

References

Marco Baroni, Silvia Bernardini, Adriano Ferraresi, and Eros Zanchetta. 2009. The wacky wide web: a collection of very large linguistically processed web-crawled corpora. *Language resources and evaluation*, 43(3):209–226.

Anja Belz, Adrian Muscat, Maxime Aberton, Sami Benjelloun, and INSA Rouen. 2015. Describing spatial relationships between objects in images in english and french. In *Proceedings of the 2015 Workshop on Vision and Language (VL'15)*, pages 104–113. Association for Comptuational Linguistics.

Patrick Blackburn and Johan Bos. 2005. *Representation and Inference for Natural Language. A First Course in Computational Semantics*. CSLI Publications.

Emmanuel Blanchard, Mounira Harzallah, Henri Briand, and Pascale Kuntz. 2005. A typology of ontology-based semantic measures. In *EMOI-INTEROP*.

Elia Bruni, Jasper Uijlings, Marco Baroni, and Nicu Sebe. 2012. Distributional semantics with eyes: Using image analysis to improve computational representations of word meaning. In *Proceedings of the 20th ACM international conference on Multimedia*, pages 1219–1228. ACM.

Bob Coyne, Richard Sproat, and Julia Hirschberg. 2010. Spatial relations in text-to-scene conversion. In *Computational Models of Spatial Language Interpretation, Workshop at Spatial Cognition*. Citeseer.

Desmond Elliott and Frank Keller. 2013. Image description using visual dependency representations. In *EMNLP*, pages 1292–1302.

Desmond Elliott, Victor Lavrenko, and Frank Keller. 2014. Query-by-example image retrieval using visual dependency representations. In *COLING 2014*, pages 109–120.

Mark Everingham and John Winn. 2012. The pascal visual object classes challenge 2012 (voc2012) development kit.

Zoe Falomir, Ernesto Jiménez-Ruiz, M Teresa Escrig, and Lledó Museros. 2011. Describing images using qualitative models and description logics. *Spatial Cognition & Computation*, 11(1):45–74.

Dirk Hovy, Taylor Berg-Kirkpatrick, Ashish Vaswani, and Eduard H Hovy. 2013. Learning whom to trust with mace. In *HLT-NAACL*, pages 1120–1130.

Andrej Karpathy and Li Fei-Fei. 2014. Deep visual-semantic alignments for generating image descriptions. *arXiv preprint arXiv:1412.2306*.

Girish Kulkarni, Visruth Premraj, Sagnik Dhar, Siming Li, Yejin Choi, Alexander C Berg, and Tamara L Berg. 2011. Baby talk: Understanding and generating image descriptions. In *Proceedings of the 24th CVPR*. Citeseer.

Angeliki Lazaridou, Dat Tien Nguyen, Raffaella Bernardi, and Marco Baroni. 2015. Unveiling the dreams of word embeddings: Towards language-driven image generation. *arXiv preprint arXiv:1506.03500*.

Mateusz Malinowski and Mario Fritz. 2014. A multiworld approach to question answering about realworld scenes based on uncertain input. In *Advances in Neural Information Processing Systems*, pages 1682–1690.

Tomas Mikolov, Kai Chen, Greg Corrado, and Jeffrey Dean. 2013a. Efficient estimation of word representations in vector space. *arXiv preprint arXiv:1301.3781*.

Tomas Mikolov, Ilya Sutskever, Kai Chen, Greg S Corrado, and Jeff Dean. 2013b. Distributed representations of words and phrases and their compositionality. In *Advances in neural information processing systems*, pages 3111–3119.

George A Miller. 1995. Wordnet: a lexical database for english. *Communications of the ACM*, 38(11):39–41.

Bernd Neumann and Ralf Möller. 2008. On scene interpretation with description logics. *Image and Vision Computing*, 26(1):82–101.

Benjamin Rosman and Subramanian Ramamoorthy. 2011. Learning spatial relationships between objects. *The International Journal of Robotics Research*, 30(11):1328–1342.

Kristoffer Sjöö, Alper Aydemir, and Patric Jensfelt. 2012. Topological spatial relations for active visual search. *Robotics and Autonomous Systems*, 60(9):1093–1107.

Oriol Vinyals, Alexander Toshev, Samy Bengio, and Dumitru Erhan. 2014. Show and tell: A neural image caption generator. *arXiv preprint arXiv:1411.4555*.

Ying-Hong Wang. 2003. Image indexing and similarity retrieval based on spatial relationship model. *Information Sciences*, 154(1):39–58.

Yezhou Yang, Ching Lik Teo, Hal Daumé III, and Yiannis Aloimonos. 2011. Corpus-guided sentence generation of natural images. In *Proceedings of the Conference on Empirical Methods in Natural Language Processing*, pages 444–454. Association for Computational Linguistics.

Yuke Zhu, Alireza Fathi, and Li Fei-Fei. 2014. Reasoning about object affordances in a knowledge base representation. In *Computer Vision–ECCV 2014*, pages 408–424. Springer.

Focused Evaluation for Image Description with Binary Forced-Choice Tasks

Micah Hodosh and **Julia Hockenmaier**
Department of Computer Science, University of Illinois
Urbana, IL 61801, USA
{mhodosh2, juliahmr}@illinois.edu

Abstract

Current evaluation metrics for image description may be too coarse. We therefore propose a series of binary forced-choice tasks that each focus on a different aspect of the captions. We evaluate a number of different off-the-shelf image description systems. Our results indicate strengths and shortcomings of both generation and ranking based approaches.

1 Introduction

Image description, i.e. the task of automatically associating photographs with sentences that describe what is depicted in them, has been framed in two different ways: as a natural language generation problem (where each system produces novel captions, see e.g. Kulkarni et al. (2011)), and as a ranking task (where each system is required to rank the same pool of unseen test captions for each test image, see e.g. Hodosh et al. (2013)).

But although the numbers reported in the literature make it seem as though this task is quickly approaching being solved (on the recent MSCOCO challenge,[1] the best models outperformed humans according to some metrics), evaluation remains problematic for both approaches (Hodosh, 2015).

Caption generation requires either automated metrics (Papineni et al., 2002; Lin, 2004; Denkowski and Lavie, 2014; Vedantam et al., 2015), most of which have been shown to correlate poorly with human judgments (Hodosh et al., 2013; Elliott and Keller, 2014; Hodosh, 2015) and fail to capture the variety in human captions, while human evaluation is subjective (especially when reduced to simple questions such as "Which is a better caption?"), expensive, and difficult to replicate. Ranking-based evaluation suffers from the

problem that the pool of candidate captions may, on the one hand, be too small to contain many meaningful and interesting distractors, and may, on the other hand, contain other sentences that are equally valid descriptions of the image.

To illustrate just how much is still to be done in this field, this paper examines a series of binary forced-choice tasks that are each designed to evaluate a particular aspect of image description. Items in each task consist of one image, paired with one correct and one incorrect caption; the system has to choose the correct caption over the distractor. These tasks are inspired both by ranking-based evaluations of image description as well as by more recent work on visual question answering (e.g. Antol et al. (2015)), but differ from these in that the negatives are far more restricted and focused than in the generic ranking task. Since most of our tasks are simple enough that they could be solved by a very simple decision rule, our aim is not to examine whether models could be trained specifically for these tasks. Instead, we wish to use these tasks to shed light on which aspects of image captions these models actually "understand", and how models trained for generation differ from models trained for ranking. The models we compare consist of a number of simple baselines, as well as some publicly available models that each had close to state-of-the-art performance on standard tasks when they were published. More details and discussion can be found in Hodosh (2015).

2 A framework for focused evaluation

In this paper, we evaluate image description systems with a series of binary (two-alternative) forced choice tasks. The items in each task consist of one image from the test or development part of the Flickr30K dataset (Young et al., 2014), paired

---

[1] http://mscoco.org/dataset/#captions-challenge2015

19

Proceedings of the 5th Workshop on Vision and Language, pages 19–28,
Berlin, Germany, August 12 2016. ©2016 Association for Computational Linguistics

"Switch People" Task		
Image	**Gold Caption**	**Distractor**
	a man holding and kissing **a crying little boy** on the cheek	**a crying little boy** holding and kissing **a man** on the cheek
	a woman is hula hooping in front of **an audience**	**an audience** is hula hooping in front of **a woman**

Figure 1: The **"switch people"** task

"Replace Scene" Task		
Image	**Gold Caption**	**Distractor**
	two dogs playing on **a beach**	two dogs playing on **frozen tundra**
	a brown dog is bending down trying to drink from **a jet of water**	a brown dog is bending down trying to drink from **your local brewery**
	a man in **a restaurant** having lunch	a man in **an office boardroom** having lunch

Figure 2: The **"replace scene"** task

with one correct and one incorrect caption, and the system has to choose (i.e. assign a higher score to) the correct caption over the distractor.

The correct caption is either an original caption or a part of an original caption for the image. Distractors are shorter phrases that occur in the original caption, complete captions for different images that share some aspect of the correct caption, or are artificially constructed sentences based on the original caption. While all distractors are constructed around the people or scene mentions in the original caption, each task is designed to focus on a particular aspect of image description. We focus on scene and people mentions because both occur frequently in Flickr30K. Unlike MSCOCO, all images in Flickr30K focus on events and activities involving people or animals. Scene terms (*"beach"*, *"city"*, *"office"*, *"street"*, *"park"*) tend to describe very visual, unlocalized components that can often be identified by the overall layout or other global properties of the image. At the same time, they restrict what kind of entities and events are likely to occur in the image. For instance, people do not "run" , "jump", or "swim" in an "office". Hence, models trained and tested on standard caption datasets do not necessarily need to model what "jumping in an office" might look like. We therefore suspect that much of the generic ranking task can be solved by identifying the visual appearance of scene terms.

Some tasks require the system to choose between two captions that provide similar descriptions of the main actor or the scene. In others, the distractor is not a full sentence, but consists only of the main actor or scene description. We also evaluate a converse task in which the distractor describes the scene correctly (but everything else in the sentence is wrong), while the correct answer consists only of the NP that describes the scene. Finally, we consider a task in which the distractor swaps two people mentions, reversing their corresponding semantic roles while keeping the same vocabulary.

3 Our tasks

Our first task (**switch people**, Fig. 1) identifies the extent to which models are able to distinguish sentences that share the same vocabulary but convey different semantic information. In this task, the correct sentences contain one person mention as the main actor and another person mention that occupies a different semantic role (e.g. "*A man holding a child*"). The distractors ("*A child holding a man*") are artificially constructed sentences in which those two people mentions are swapped. This allows us to evaluate whether models can capture semantically important differences in word order, even when the bag-of-words representation of two captions is identical (and bag-of-words-based evaluation metrics such as BLEU1, ROUGE1 or CIDER would not be able to capture the difference either).

In the **replace person** and **replace scene** task (Fig. 2), distractors are artificially constructed sentences in which the main actor (the first person mention) or the scene chunk (which typically occurs at the end of the sentence) were replaced by different people or scene mentions. These tasks

"Share Scene" Task		
Image	**GoldCaption**	**Distractor**
	a man in a suit and tie in a fancy building is speaking at **the podium**	a lady is giving a speech at **the podium**
	there is a woman riding a bike down **the road** and she popped a wheelie	two men in jeans and jackets are walking down **a small road**

Figure 3: The **"share scene"** task

"Just Person" Task		
Image	**Gold Caption**	**Distractor**

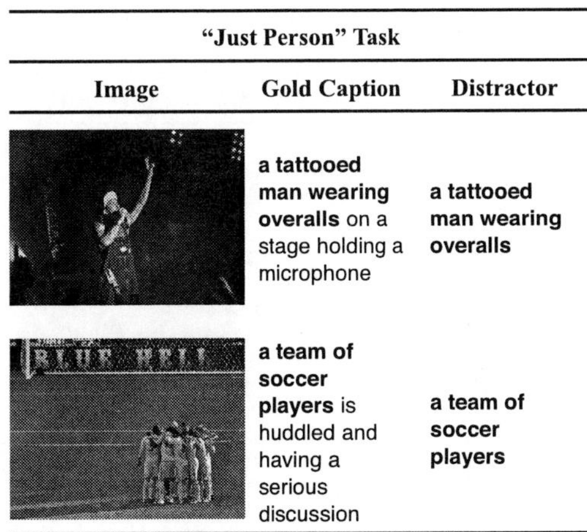

	a tattooed man wearing overalls on a stage holding a microphone	**a tattooed man wearing overalls**
	a team of soccer players is huddled and having a serious discussion	**a team of soccer players**

Figure 4: The **"just person"** task

aim to elicit how much systems are able to identify correct person or scene descriptions. Models should be able to understand when a person is being described incorrectly, even when the rest of the sentence remains correct. Similarly, since the scene is important to the overall understanding of the a caption, we wanted to make sure models grasp that changing the scene terms of a caption can drastically change its meaning.

The **share person** and **share scene** distractors (Fig. 3) are complete sentences from the training portion of Flickr30K whose actor or scene mentions share the same headword as the correct description for the test image. These tasks aim to elicit the extent to which systems focus only on the person or scene descriptions, while ignoring the rest of the sentence.

We also evaluate whether models are able to identify when a complete sentence is a better description of an image than a single NP. The **just person** and **just scene** distractors (Figs. 4 and 5) are NPs that consist only of the person or scene mentions of the correct description, and aim to identify whether systems prefer more detailed (correct) descriptions over shorter (but equally correct) ones. Finally, since systems can perform well on these tasks by simply preferring longer captions, we also developed a converse **just scene (+)** task, which pairs the (short, but correct) scene description with a (longer, but incorrect) sentence that shares the same scene.

3.1 Task construction

All our tasks are constructed around people and scene mentions, based on the chunking and the dictionaries provided in Plummer et al. (2015). Person mentions are NP chunks whose head noun

refer to people (*"a tall man"*) or groups of people (*"a football team"*), or "NP1-of-NP2" constructions where the head of the first NP is a collective noun and the head of the second NP refers to people (*"a group of protesters"*). Subsequent NP chunks that refer to clothing are also included (*"a girl in jeans"*, *"a team in blue"*. Scene mentions are NP chunks whose head noun refers to locations (e.g. *"beach"*, *"city"*, *"office"*, *"street"*, *"park"*).

Switch people task We start with all captions of the 1000 development images that contain two distinct people mentions (excluding near-identical phrase pairs such as *"one man"*/*"another man"*). We filtered out examples in which the grammatical role reversal is semantically equivalent to the original (*"A man talking with a woman"*). Since we wished to maintain identical bag-of-words representations (to avoid differences between the captions that are simply due to different token frequencies) while focusing on examples that still remain grammatically correct (to minimize the effect of evaluating just how well a model generates or scores grammatically correct English text), we also excluded captions where one mention (e.g. the subject) is singular and the other (e.g. an object) is plural. When swapping two mentions, we also include the subsequent clothing chunks (e.g. *"man in red sweater"*) in addition to other pre-modifiers (*"a tall man"*). We automatically generate and hand prune a list of the possible permutations of the person chunks, resulting in 296 sentence pairs to use for evaluation.

"Just Scene" Task		
Image	**Gold Caption**	**Distractor**
	a man sleeping in **a green room** on a couch	**a green room**
	a lady is sitting down tending to **her stand**	**her stand**
	a child poses wearing glasses near **water** outside	**water**

Figure 5: The **"just scene"** task

Replace person/scene tasks For the "replace person" task, we isolate person chunks, in both the training and development data. For each development sentence, we create a distractor by replacing each person chunk with a random chunk from the training data, resulting in 5816 example pairs to evaluate. For the "replace scene" task we created negative examples by replacing the scene chunk of a caption with another scene chunk from the data. Because multiple surface strings can describe the same overall scene, we use the training corpus to calculate which scene chunk's headwords can co-occur in the training corpus. We avoid all such replacements in order to ensure that the negative sentence does not actually still describe the image. In theory, this should be a baseline that all state-of-the-art image description models excel at.

Share person/scene tasks Here, the distractors consist of sentences from the Flickr30K training data which describe a similar main actor or scene as the correct caption. For each sentence in the development data, we chose a random training sentence that shares the same headword for its "actor" chunk, resulting in 4595 items to evaluate. We did the same for development sentences that mention a scene term, resulting in 2620 items.

Just person/scene tasks Finally, the "just person" and "just scene" tasks require the models to pick a complete sentence (again taken from the development set) over a shorter noun phrase that is a substring of the correct answer, consisting of either the main actor or the scene description. Although the distractors are not wrong, they typi-

cally only convey a very limited amount of information about the image, and models should prefer the more detailed descriptions provided by the complete sentences, as long as they are also correct. But since these tasks can be solved perfectly by any model that consistently prefers longer captions over shorter ones, we also investigate a converse "just scene (+)" task; here the correct answer is a noun phrase describing the scene, while the distractor is another full sentence that contains the same scene word (as in the "share scene" task). Taken together, these tasks allow us to evaluate the extent to which models rely solely on the person or scene description and ignore the rest of the sentence.

4 The Models

We evaluate generation and ranking models that were publicly available and relatively close in performance to state of the art, as well as two simple baselines.

Generation models Our baseline model for generation (**Bigram LM**) ignores the image entirely. It returns the caption that has a higher probability according to an unsmoothed bigram language model estimated over the sentences in the training portion of the Flickr30K corpus.

As an example of an actual generation model for image description, we evaluate a publicly available implementation[2] of the generation model originally presented by Vinyals et al. (2015) (**Generation**).   This model uses an LSTM (Hochreiter and Schmidhuber, 1997) conditioned on the image to generate new captions. The particular instance we evaluate was trained on the MSCOCO dataset (Lin et al., 2014), not Flickr30K (leading to a possible decrease in performance on our tasks) and uses VGGNet (Simonyan and Zisserman, 2014) image features (which should account for a significant jump in performance over the previously published results of Vinyals et al. (2015)). Works such as Vinyals et al. (2015) and Mao et al. (2014) present models that are developed for the generation task, but renormalize the probability that their models assign to sentences when they apply them to ranking tasks (even though their models include stop probabilities that should enable them to directly compare sentences of different lengths). To examine the ef-

---

[2] http://cs.stanford.edu/people/karpathy/neuraltalk/

fect of such normalization schemes, we also consider normalized variants of our two generation models in which we replace the original sentence probabilities by their harmonic mean. We will see that the unnormalized versions of these models tend to perform poorly when the gold caption is measurably longer than the distractor term, and well in the reverse case, while normalization attempts to counteract this trend.

Ranking models Ranking models learn embeddings of images and captions in the same space, and score the affinity of images and captions in terms of their Euclidian distance in this space. We compare the performance of these generation models with two (updated) versions of the ranking model originally presented by Kiros et al. (2014)[3] (**LSTM Ranking**), one trained on MSCOCO, and the other on Flickr30K. This model uses an LSTM to learn the embedding of the captions. While the Flickr30K trained model should be more appropriate for our test data, the MSCOCO trained model might be more directly comparable to the generation model of Vinyals et al. A comparison between the two variants can offer insight into the degree of domain shift between the two datasets.

Our ranking baseline model (**BOW Ranking**) replaces the LSTM of Kiros et al. (2014) with a simple bag-of-words text representation, allowing us to examine whether the expressiveness of LSTMs is required for this task. We use the average of the tokens' GloVe embeddings (Pennington et al., 2014) as input to a fully connected neural network layer that produces the final learned text embedding[4]. More formally, for a sentence consisting of tokens $w_1...w_n$, GloVe embeddings $\phi()$, and a non-linear activation function σ_w, we define the learned sentence embedding as $F(w_1...w_n) = \sigma_w(W_w \cdot (\frac{1}{n}) \sum_i \phi(w_i) + b_w)$. Similarly, the embedding of an image represented as a vector p is defined as $G(p) = \sigma_i(W_i \cdot p + b_i)$. We use a ranking loss similar to Kiros et al. (2014) to train the parameters of our model, $\theta = (W_w, W_i, b_w, b_i)$. We define the distance of the embeddings of image i and sentence s as $\Delta(i,s) = \cos(F(i), G(s))$. Using S to refer to the set of sentences in the training data, S_i for the training sentences associated with image i, S_{-i} for the set of sentences not associated with i, I for the set of training images, I_s

for the image associated with sentence s, and I_{-s} for the set of all other training images, and employing a free parameter m for the margin of the ranking, our loss function is:

$$L(\theta) = \sum_{i \in I, s \in S_i, s' \in S_{-i}} \max(0, m - \Delta(i,s) + \Delta(i,s')) \\ + \sum_{s \in S, i \in I_s, i' \in I_{-s}} \max(0, m - \Delta(i,s)) + \Delta(i',s)))$$

As input image features, we used the 19 layer VGGNet features (Simonyan and Zisserman, 2014), applied as by Plummer et al. (2015). We first process the GloVe embeddings by performing whitening through zero-phase component analysis (ZCA) (Coates and Ng, 2012) based on every token appearance in our training corpus. We set σ_w to be a ReLU and simply use the identity function for σ_i (i.e. no non-linearity) as that resulted in the best validation performance. We train this model on the Flickr30K training data via stochastic gradient descent, randomly sampling either 50 images (or sentences), and randomly sampling one of the other training sentences (images). We adjust the learning rate of each parameter using Adagrad (Duchi et al., 2010) with an initial learning rate of 0.01, a momentum value of 0.8, and a parameter decay value of 0.0001 for regularization.

5 Results

Results for all tasks can be found in Table 1.

The "switch people" task The generation models are much better than the ranking models at capturing the difference in word order that distinguishes the correct answer from the distractor in this task. At 52% accuracy, the ranking models perform only marginally better than the ranking baseline model, which ignores word order, and therefore performs at chance. But the 69% accuracy obtained by the generation models is about the same as the performance of the bigram baseline that ignores the image. This indicates that neither of the models actually "understands" the sentences (e.g. the difference between men carrying children and children carrying men), although generation models perform significantly better than chance because they are often able to distinguish the more common phrases that occur in the correct answers ("man carries child") from those that appear in the constructed sentences that serve as distractors here ("child carries man"). It

---

[3] https://github.com/ryankiros/visual-semantic-embedding
[4] Deeper and more complex representations showed no conclusive benefit

# of pairs	Switch People 296	Replace Person 5816	Replace Scene 2513	Share Person 4595	Share Scene 2620	Just Person 5811	Just Scene 2624	Just Scene(+) 2620
Bigram LM	**69.8**	83.0	77.5	49.6	47.9	1.1	0.0	**99.6**
Normalized Bigram LM	**69.8**	69.9	76.5	50.2	50.9	31.3	28.2	71.0
Generation (COCO)	69.3	**85.2**	85.2	56.5	54.7	3.8	7.4	94.2
Normalized Generation (COCO)	68.9	74.0	85.5	61.6	59.2	79.5	**97.3**	5.5
BOW Ranking (Flickr30K)	50.0	84.9	**89.3**	**93.6**	**89.9**	81.2	84.6	71.3
LSTM Ranking (COCO)	52.0	79.4	86.6	89.9	88.0	79.8	86.5	58.2
LSTM Ranking (Flickr30K)	52.0	81.1	87.0	92.5	89.3	**82.6**	78.8	75.5

Table 1: Accuracies of the different models on our tasks

seems that localization of entities (Plummer et al., 2015; Xu et al., 2015) may be required to address this issue and go beyond baseline performance.

The "replace person/scene" tasks On the "replace person" task, the (unnormalized) bigram baseline has a relatively high accuracy of 83%, perhaps because the distractors are again artificially constructed sentences. The ranking baseline model and the (unnormalized) generation model outperform this baseline somewhat at around 85%, while the ranking models perform below the bigram baseline. The ranking model trained on Flickr30K has a slight advantage over the same model trained on MSCOCO, an (unsurprising) difference that also manifests itself in the remaining tasks, but both models perform below the ranking baseline. Normalization hurts both generation models significantly. It is instructive to compare performance on this task with the "replace scene" task. We see again that normalization hurts for generation, while the baseline ranking model outperforms the more sophisticated version. But here, all models that consider the image outperform the bigram model by a very clear eight to almost twelve percent. This indicates that all image description models that we consider here rely heavily on scene or global image features. It would be interesting to see whether models that use explicit object detectors could overcome this bias.

The "share person/scene" tasks The distractors in these tasks are captions for other images that share the same actor or scene head noun. Since the bigram language models ignore the image, they cannot distinguish the two cases (it is unclear why the unnormalized bigram model's accuracy on the "share scene" task is not closer to fifty percent). And while normalization helps the generation model a little, its accuracies of 61.6% and 59.2% are far below those of the ranking mod-

els, indicating that the latter are much better at distinguishing between the correct caption and an equally fluent, but incorrect one. This is perhaps not surprising, since this task is closest to the ranking loss that these models are trained to optimize. By focusing on an adversarial ranking loss between training captions, the ranking model may be able to more correctly pick up important subtle differences between in-domain images, while the generation model is not directly optimized for this task (and instead has to also capture other properties of the captions, e.g. fluency). With an accuracy of 93.6% and 89.9%, the bag-of-word ranking baseline model again outperforms the more complex LSTM. But examining its errors is informative. In general, it appears that it makes errors when examples require more subtle understanding or are atypical images for the words in the caption, as shown in Figure 6.

The "just person/scene" tasks The "just person" and "just scene" tasks differ from all other tasks we consider in that the distractors are also correct descriptions of the image, although they are consistently shorter. To actually solve these tasks, models should be able to identify that the additional information provided in the longer caption is correct. By contrast, the "just scene (+)" task requires them to identify that the additional information provided in the longer caption is not correct. But a simple preference for longer or shorter captions can also go a long way towards "solving" these tasks. In this case, we would expect to see a model's performance on the "just scene" task to be close to the complement of its performance on the converse "just scene (+)" task. This is indeed the case for the bigram and the generation models (but not for the ranking models). This preference is particularly obvious in the case of the unnormalized bigram model (which

Image	Gold Caption	Distractor: Shares a Scene
	a group of children in the ocean (0.194)	a person in a kayak rides waves in the ocean (0.344)
	two women are sitting in ditches of dirt with two buckets and a purse close by (0.378)	the young toddlers is dressed in yellow and purple while sitting on the ground with three bucks filling them with dirt (0.393)
	a group of people hold hands on the beach (0.609)	a group of people are lounging at a beach (0.613)
	a dog drags a white rag through an almost dried up creek (0.330)	a dog jumps over a creek (0.433)

Figure 6: Examples from the "share scene" task that the BOW ranking model gets wrong, together with its scores for each of the captions.

does not take the image into account), and, to a slightly lesser extent, by the unnormalized generation model (which does). Both models have near perfect accuracy on the "just scene (+)" task, and near complete failure on the other two tasks. Length normalization reduces this preference for shorter captions somewhat in the case of the bigram model, and seems to simply reverse it for the generation model. None of the ranking models show such a marked preference for either long or short captions. But although each model has similar accuracies on the "just scene" and on the "just scene (+)" task, accuracies on the "just scene" task are higher than on the "just scene (+)" task. This indicates that they are not always able to identify when the additional information is incorrect (as in the "just scene (+)" task). Accuracies on the "just person" task tend to be lower, but are otherwise generally comparable to those on the "just scene" task. We see the biggest drops for the length-normalized generation model, whose accuracy goes down from 97.3% on the scene task to 79.5% (indicating that something else besides a preference for longer captions is at play), and the MSCOCO-trained ranking model which goes down from 86.5% to 79.8%.

It is unclear why the performance on the "just person" task tends to be lower than on the "just scene" task. Since scenes correspond to global image properties, we stipulate that models are better at identifying them than most people terms. Although some people descriptions (e.g. "baseball player", "audience") are highly indicative of the scene, this is not the case for very generic terms ("man", "woman"). We also note that identifying when the additional information is correct can be quite difficult. For example, in the second example in Figure 4, the phrase "huddled and having a serious discussion" has to be understood in the context of soccer. While the dataset contains other images of discussions, there are no other instances of discussions taking place on soccer fields, and the people in those cases tend to occupy a much larger portion of the image. Further analyzing and isolating these examples (and similar ones) is key for future progress. Figure 7 shows items from the "just scene" task that the BOW model gets right, paired with items for the same image where it makes a mistake. For the first item, it seems that the model associates the terms "crowd" or "crowded" with this image (while not understanding that "busy" is synonymous with "crowded" in this context). The error on the second item may be due to the word "rock" in the correct answer (Flickr30K contains a lot of images of rock climbing), while the error on the fourth item may be due to the use of words like "parents" rather than the more generic "people."

5.1 Discussion

We compared generation models for image description, which are trained to produce fluent descriptions of the image, with ranking-based models, which learn to embed images and captions in a common space in such a way that captions appear near the images they describe. Among the models we were able to evaluate, ranking-based approaches outperformed generation-based ones on most tasks, and a simple bag-of-words models per-

Image	Gold Caption	Distractor: A Scene Chunk
	a single man in a black tshirt standing above the crowd at a busy bar (0.329)	a busy bar (0.203)
	a man is making a rock gesture while standing on a stool in a crowded bar (0.216)	**a crowded bar (0.327)**
	some people in formal attire stand in front of the altar in a church sanctuary (0.434)	a church sanctuary (0.325)
	a son and his parents are taking a group picture in a church (0.274)	**a church (0.399)**

Figure 7: Items from the "Just Scene" task with the scores from the BOW ranking model in parentheses (bold = the caption preferred by the model).

formed similarly to a comparable LSTM model.

The "switch people" results indicate that ranking models may not capture subtle semantic differences created by changing the word order of the original caption (i.e. swapping subjects and objects). But although generation models seem to perform much better on this task, their accuracy is only as good as, or even slightly lower than, that of a simple bigram language model that ignores the image. This indicates that generation models may have simply learned to distinguish between plausible and implausible sentences.

The "share person/scene" and "just person/scene" results indicate that ranking models may be better at capturing subtle details of the image than generation models. But our results also indicate that both kinds of models still have a long way to before they are able to describe images accurately with a "human level of detail."

Our comparison of the LSTM-based model of Kiros et al. (2014) against our bag-of-words baseline model indicates that the former may not be taking advantage of the added representational power of LSTMs (in fact, most of the recent improvements on this task may be largely due to the use of better vision features and dense word embeddings trained on large corpora). However, RNNs (Elman, 1990) and LSTMs offer convenient ways to define a probability distribution across the space of all possible image captions that cannot be modeled as easily with a bag-of-words style approach. The question remains if that convenience comes at a cost of no longer being able to easily train a model that understands the language to an acceptable amount of detail. It is also important to note that we were unable to evaluate a model that combines a generation model with a reranker such Fang et al. (2014) and the follow up work in Devlin et al. (2015). In theory, if the generation models are able produce a significantly enough diverse set of captions, the reranking can make up the gap in performance while still being able to generate novel captions easily.

6 Conclusion

It is clear that evaluation still remains a difficult issue for image description. The community needs to develop metrics that are more sensitive than the ranking task while being more directly correlated to human judgement than current automated metrics used for generation. In this paper, we developed a sequence of binary forced-choice tasks to evaluate and compare different models for image description. Our results indicate that generation and ranking-based approaches are both far from having "solved" this task, and that each approach has different advantages and deficiencies. But the aim of this study was less to analyze the behavior of specific models (we simply used models whose performance was close to state of the art, and whose implementations were available to us) than to highlight issues that are not apparent under current evaluation metrics, and to stimulate a discussion about what kind of evaluation methods are appropriate for this burgeoning area. Our data is available,[5] and will allow others to evaluate their models directly.

---

[5] http://nlp.cs.illinois.edu/HockenmaierGroup/data.html

Acknowledgments

This paper is based upon work supported by the National Science Foundation under Grants No. 1205627, 1405883 and 1053856. Any opinions, findings, and conclusions or recommendations expressed in this material are those of the author(s) and do not necessarily reflect the views of the National Science Foundation.

References

Stanislaw Antol, Aishwarya Agrawal, Jiasen Lu, Margaret Mitchell, Dhruv Batra, C. Lawrence Zitnick, and Devi Parikh. 2015. VQA: visual question answering. In *2015 IEEE International Conference on Computer Vision, ICCV 2015*, pages 2425–2433.

Adam Coates and Andrew Y. Ng. 2012. Learning feature representations with k-means. In *Neural Networks: Tricks of the Trade - Second Edition*, pages 561–580.

Michael Denkowski and Alon Lavie. 2014. Meteor universal: Language specific translation evaluation for any target language. In *Proceedings of the EACL 2014 Workshop on Statistical Machine Translation*.

Jacob Devlin, Hao Cheng, Hao Fang, Saurabh Gupta, Li Deng, Xiaodong He, Geoffrey Zweig, and Margaret Mitchell. 2015. Language models for image captioning: The quirks and what works. In *Proceedings of the 53rd Annual Meeting of the Association for Computational Linguistics and the 7th International Joint Conference on Natural Language Processing of the Asian Federation of Natural Language Processing, ACL 2015, Volume 2: Short Papers*, pages 100–105.

John Duchi, Elad Hazan, and Yoram Singer. 2010. Adaptive subgradient methods for online learning and stochastic optimization. Technical Report UCB/EECS-2010-24, EECS Department, University of California, Berkeley, Mar.

Desmond Elliott and Frank Keller. 2014. Comparing automatic evaluation measures for image description. In *Proceedings of the 52nd Annual Meeting of the Association for Computational Linguistics (Volume 2: Short Papers)*, pages 452–457, Baltimore, Maryland, June.

Jeffrey L. Elman. 1990. Finding structure in time. *Cognitive Science*, 14(2):179–211.

Hao Fang, Saurabh Gupta, Forrest N. Iandola, Rupesh Srivastava, Li Deng, Piotr Dollár, Jianfeng Gao, Xiaodong He, Margaret Mitchell, John C. Platt, C. Lawrence Zitnick, and Geoffrey Zweig. 2014. From captions to visual concepts and back. *CoRR*, abs/1411.4952.

Sepp Hochreiter and Jürgen Schmidhuber. 1997. Long short-term memory. *Neural Computation*, 9(8):1735–1780, November.

Micah Hodosh, Peter Young, and Julia Hockenmaier. 2013. Framing image description as a ranking task: Data, models and evaluation metrics. *Journal of Artifical Intellegence*, 47:853–899.

Micah Hodosh. 2015. *Natural language image description: data, models, and evaluation*. Ph.D. thesis, University of Illinois.

Ryan Kiros, Ruslan Salakhutdinov, and Richard S. Zemel. 2014. Unifying visual-semantic embeddings with multimodal neural language models. *CoRR*, abs/1411.2539.

Girish Kulkarni, Visruth Premraj, Sagnik Dhar, Siming Li, Yejin Choi, Alexander C. Berg, and Tamara L. Berg. 2011. Baby talk: Understanding and generating simple image descriptions. In *Proceedings of the 2011 IEEE Conference on Computer Vision and Pattern Recognition (CVPR)*, pages 1601–1608.

Tsung-Yi Lin, Michael Maire, Serge Belongie, James Hays, Pietro Perona, Deva Ramanan, Piotr Dollár, and C. Lawrence Zitnick. 2014. Microsoft COCO: Common objects in context. In *European Conference on Computer Vision (ECCV)*.

Chin-Yew Lin. 2004. Rouge: A package for automatic evaluation of summaries. In Stan Szpakowicz Marie-Francine Moens, editor, *Text Summarization Branches Out: Proceedings of the ACL-04 Workshop*, pages 74–81, Barcelona, Spain, July.

Junhua Mao, Wei Xu, Yi Yang, Jiang Wang, and Alan L. Yuille. 2014. Deep captioning with multimodal recurrent neural networks (m-rnn). *CoRR*, abs/1412.6632.

Kishore Papineni, Salim Roukos, Todd Ward, and Wei-Jing Zhu. 2002. Bleu: a method for automatic evaluation of machine translation. In *Proceedings of 40th Annual Meeting of the Association for Computational Linguistics (ACL)*, pages 311–318, July.

Jeffrey Pennington, Richard Socher, and Christopher Manning. 2014. Glove: Global vectors for word representation. In *Proceedings of the 2014 Conference on Empirical Methods in Natural Language Processing (EMNLP)*, pages 1532–1543, Doha, Qatar, October. Association for Computational Linguistics.

Bryan A. Plummer, Liwei Wang, Chris M. Cervantes, Juan C. Caicedo, Julia Hockenmaier, and Svetlana Lazebnik. 2015. Flickr30k Entities: collecting region-to-phrase correspondences for richer image-to-sentence models. In *The IEEE International Conference on Computer Vision (ICCV)*, December.

K. Simonyan and A. Zisserman. 2014. Very deep convolutional networks for large-scale image recognition. *CoRR*, abs/1409.1556.

Ramakrishna Vedantam, C. Lawrence Zitnick, and Devi Parikh. 2015. CIDEr: Consensus-based image description evaluation. In *IEEE Conference on Computer Vision and Pattern Recognition, CVPR 2015*, pages 4566–4575.

Oriol Vinyals, Alexander Toshev, Samy Bengio, and Dumitru Erhan. 2015. Show and tell: A neural image caption generator. In *IEEE Conference on Computer Vision and Pattern Recognition, CVPR 2015*, pages 3156–3164.

Kelvin Xu, Jimmy Ba, Ryan Kiros, Kyunghyun Cho, Aaron C. Courville, Ruslan Salakhutdinov, Richard S. Zemel, and Yoshua Bengio. 2015. Show, attend and tell: Neural image caption generation with visual attention. *CoRR*, abs/1502.03044.

Peter Young, Alice Lai, Micah Hodosh, and Julia Hockenmaier. 2014. From image descriptions to visual denotations: New similarity metrics for semantic inference over event descriptions. *Transactions of the Association for Computational Linguistics*, 2:67–78.

Leveraging Captions in the Wild to Improve Object Detection

Mert Kilickaya, Nazli Ikizler-Cinbis, Erkut Erdem and Aykut Erdem
Department of Computer Engineering
Hacettepe University
Beytepe, Ankara
`kilickayamert@gmail.com`
`{nazli, erkut, aykut}@cs.hacettepe.edu.tr`

Abstract

In this study, we explore whether the captions in the wild can boost the performance of object detection in images. Captions that accompany images usually provide significant information about the visual content of the image, making them an important resource for image understanding. However, captions in the wild are likely to include numerous types of noises which can hurt visual estimation. In this paper, we propose data-driven methods to deal with the noisy captions and utilize them to improve object detection. We show how a pre-trained state-of-the-art object detector can take advantage of noisy captions. Our experiments demonstrate that captions provide promising cues about the visual content of the images and can aid in improving object detection.

1 Introduction

Visual data on the Internet is generally coupled with descriptive text such as tags, keywords or captions. While tags and keywords are typically composed of single words, or phrases, and generally depict the main entities in an image (e.g. objects, places, etc.), a caption is a complete sentence which is intended to describe the image in a holistic manner. It can reveal information about not just the existing objects or the corresponding event but also the relationships between the objects/scene elements, their attributes or the actions in a scene (Figure 1). In this respect, captions provide a much richer source of information in order to understand the image content. This has recently motivated researchers to automate the task of describing images in natural languages using captions (Raffaella et al., 2016). However, most of these studies employ carefully collected image descriptions which are obtained by services like Amazon's Mechanical Turk (Rashtchian et al., 2010a; Hodosh et al., 2013; Young et al., 2014a; Lin et al., 2014). Little has been done on utilizing captions in the wild, i.e. the captions that accompany images readily available on the Web.

Although captions are rich, there are some challenges that limit their use in computer vision, and related language tasks. First, a caption may not be a visual depiction of the scene, but rather a sort of comment not directly related to the visual content of the image (Figure 1). The users might avoid explaining the obvious, but talk about more indirect aspects, abstract concepts and/or feelings. Third, the caption may be poorly written, which makes it difficult to understand the meaning of the text associated with the image.

On the other hand, there is also a major advantage in having image-caption pairs on the Web; billions of them are freely available online. Collectively considering image-caption pairs associated with a certain query image may allow to eliminate noisy information. Researchers have used this idea to collect a large scale images-captions dataset consisting of clean, descriptive texts paired with images (Chen et al., 2015). When noisy captions are eliminated, the rest can serve as an excellent source of information for what is available in the visual world.

In this paper, we investigate whether we can leverage captions in the wild to improve object detection. Object detection has seen some significant advances in recent years thanks to convolutional neural networks (LeCun et al., 2015). But in some cases, even state-of-the-art object detectors may fail to accurately locate objects or may produce false positives (see Figure 2). For such situations, we propose to utilize captions as an alternative source of information to determine what

29

Proceedings of the 5th Workshop on Vision and Language, pages 29–38,
Berlin, Germany, August 12 2016. ©2016 Association for Computational Linguistics

the big yellow horse in Prague

beautiful young woman sitting near her bicycle under the tree in forest with map in her hands

above clouds airplane window (10)

Hey diddle diddle... the cat and the fiddle... the cow jumped over the M00N!!

Figure 1: Left: Examples of good captions, carrying rich information about the visual content of the image such as existence, sizes, attributes of objects, or their spatial organization. Right: Examples of noisy captions, where the mentioned objects may not exist visually (magenta for existing, red for non-existing objects).

is present in the image. Due to the reasons stated above, however, leveraging captions directly may result in errors. Therefore, we suggest to use data-driven methods which can eliminate the noise in the captions and inform about which objects are available in the image.

For our purpose, we first consider a constrained scenario where we assume access to test image captions and run detectors for objects mentioned in the caption, as previously motivated by (Ordonez et al., 2015). Then, we proceed to explore a more general setting where we observe captions only at training stage and infer possible objects within the test image using similar training images and their captions. In finding similar images/captions, we propose to use three different approaches, based on nearest neighbors, 2-view Canonical Correlation Analysis (CCA) and 3-view CCA. When the visual input is combined with caption information, these approaches not only help us to eliminate the noise in the captions, but also to infer about possible objects not even mentioned in the caption of a test image (see Figure 2). Our experimental results show that utilizing noisy captions of visually similar images in the proposed ways can indeed help in improving the performance of the object detection.

2 Related Work

In this section, we briefly review some of the relevant literature related to our problem.

2.1 Employing tags and captions to improve image parsing

Image parsing refers to the process of densely assigning a class label to each pixel in an image, which traditionally requires a large set of train-

ing images with pixel-level annotations. Similar to our goals here, some recent studies have focused on exploiting image tags (Xu et al., 2014) or sentences (Fidler et al., 2013; Cheng et al., 2014) associated with images to improve the performance by using objects or attributes exist in the images.

2.2 Weakly-supervised object localization

Another line of research close to ours is weakly-supervised object localization where the training set involves image-level labels which indicate the object classes present in the images. In addition to generic object detection approaches (e.g. (Pandey and Lazebnik, 2011; Siva and Xiang, 2011; Cinbis et al., 2016)), related studies also include face recognition with supervision from captions and script (Berg et al., 2004; Everingham et al., 2009).

2.3 Text-to-image co-referencing

Motivated from co-reference resolution tasks in NLP, a number of studies have investigated matching free-form phrases with images where the task is to locate each visual entity mentioned in a caption by predicting a bounding box in the corresponding image (Hodosh et al., 2010; Kong et al., 2014; Plummer et al., 2015; Rohrbach et al., 2015).

2.4 Automatic image captioning

Image captioning aims at automatically generating a description of a query image (Raffaella et al., 2016). As opposed to recent neural models, early image captioning methods mostly follow a grounded approach and generate descriptions by first detecting objects present in the images (Ordonez et al., 2015). The main drawback with this approach, however, is that object detectors may

Caption: Probably in pursuit of a motorcycle going up on the road past our house, or similar

Figure 2: Motivation. Given an image, Faster R-CNN detects the dog successfully however also produces many false positives (Left). A naive way to incorporate the caption would be to run detectors *only* mentioned in the caption of the image (Middle). This would also lead to false detections as the photographer did not mention the dog. In our approach, we leverage several captions to estimate the candidate objects in the image, in this case, the dog (Right).

produce many false positives and moreover, not all objects are important to be mentioned in the descriptions (Berg et al., 2012).

2.5 Detecting visual text

Lastly, a few works aim at detecting visual text, i.e., understanding whether an image caption contains visually relevant phrases or not (Dodge et al., 2012; Chen et al., 2013). Here, the approach in (Dodge et al., 2012) is especially quite related to our work because it involves the subtask of running several object detectors to infer what is present in the image using information from the captions.

3 Dataset

Recent datasets for language and vision research include natural images with natural language sentences. These sentences are either the photo captions generated by the users (aka. captions in the wild) (Ordonez et al., 2015; Chen et al., 2015; Thomee et al., 2016) or the descriptions collected via crowd-sourcing (Farhadi et al., 2010; Rashtchian et al., 2010b; Young et al., 2014b; Keller et al., 2014; Lin et al., 2014; Yatskar et al., 2014; Plummer et al., 2015). Although the datasets containing the crowd-sourced descriptions, namely Pascal Sentences (Farhadi et al., 2010), Visual and Linguistic Treebank (Keller et al., 2014), Flickr30K Entities (Plummer et al., 2015), Microsoft Research Dense Visual Annotation Corpus (Yatskar et al., 2014) and MS-COCO (Lin et al., 2014) datasets have extra object-level annotations, none of the datasets that consist of user-generated captions have these kind of information. Hence, in our work, we collected a new dataset of object-level annotated images that includes captions in the wild.

We built on our dataset named SBU-Objects from (Ordonez et al., 2015) which includes 1 million Flickr images and associated captions provided by the corresponding users. Although much effort has been made to eliminate noisy, non-visual captions, an important portion of these images have sentences that do not directly describe the visual content of these images. Figure 1 demonstrates such examples. The first example includes a caption mentioning an aeroplane, but it is mentioned only because the image is captured from the window of the airplane. The second example associates an image to a figurative caption that does not describe the visual content.

We restrict ourselves to the images containing captions where the object classes from the PAS-CAL challenge (Everingham et al., 2012) are mentioned such as dog, aeroplane, car, etc. To that end, we queried the dataset considering these PAS-CAL classes as well as their synonyms (e.g., motorbike, motorcycle). We also favoured image-caption pairs that include place prepositions such as *in, on, under, front* and *behind* coupled with the query noun (e.g., dog *under* the tree) if exist. This ensures the image-caption pairs to be used for exploring the effect of spatial information in captions and images as well. We observed that captions that are short (e.g., max 4 words) or in the form

Table 1: Corpus statistics. For each object class, we provide the number of instances in the dataset and their visibility rates $p(visible|mentioned)$.

Class	dog	bottle	chair	horse	cat	d. table	bird	cow	bike	sofa
# Instances	289	79	119	289	135	69	308	255	294	289
$p(visible|mentioned)$	0.77	0.65	0.62	0.61	0.60	0.59	0.58	0.58	0.58	0.77

Class	sheep	boat	p. plant	m. bike	car	plane	monitor	bus	train
# Instances	79	119	289	135	69	308	255	294	321
$p(visible|mentioned)$	0.65	0.62	0.61	0.60	0.59	0.58	0.58	0.58	0.18

of phrases tend to be cleaner than longer captions. However, as our main aim is to leverage captions in the wild for object detection, we uniformly sampled captions that have different lengths between $[3 - 19]$ tokens, preventing the bias against caption lengths. We sampled 3.2k of such images for annotation and collected object-level bounding boxes for each and every PASCAL object available in the image. Table 1 shows the distribution of the number of object instances along with their visibility rates which is measured as the conditional probability given that a class name is mentioned in a caption, how frequent it actually exists in the image. As can be seen, animate objects like dogs, horses and cats appear frequently when mentioned while vehicles like aeroplane, bus and train have low visibilities.

4 Improving object detection with captions

In its simplest form, our aim is to determine candidate objects that can be detected from the image. Formally, given an image I_i, our aim is to estimate candidate object classes $C_i \in C$ visually present in the image, so that to eliminate false positives, only detectors of C_i are applied to the image. For simplicity, we assume that the set of possible object classes C is fixed, and the list of mentioned objects M_i is simply obtained from the captions via text-based search.

We begin with a simple, constrained scenario that assumes access to test image captions. Then, we proceed to explore more general setting where the captions are observed only at training.

4.1 Using pure captions

As stated previously, this simple model determines candidate objects directly from image's caption and hence, assumes that the caption of the image is given (at test time). This idea has previously been evaluated by (Ordonez et al., 2015) with a limited set of images for motivational purposes. Formally, given an image I_i, its caption T_i and the list of mentioned objects within that caption M_i, the candidate object classes is simply the list of mentioned objects, ie. $C_i = \{c_j, c_j \in M_i\}$.

This simple idea works surprisingly well, however, it restricts the search space for candidate objects C_i to the list of mentioned objects in the caption. The captions may be noisy, thus this procedure may suffer from typical issues stated previously; not all objects may be mentioned in the caption, and not all of the mentioned objects may be visible in the image.

4.2 Data-driven estimation of candidate objects

A more general setting is the case where we do not have access to the captions of newly seen images. Here, we describe three alternative data-driven methods for candidate object estimation.

4.2.1 Nearest-neighbor based estimation

For a given image, the captions of the visually similar images can be retrieved and utilized to identify potential object candidates. Our first method explores this approach, by directly measuring the similarity between images in visual feature space. With this setting, our aim is to see how well we can estimate candidate objects of a test image using uni-modal similarity.

To retrieve visually similar images, we need robust descriptors V that can represent the visual content effectively. To this end, we use two alternatives; first is the *fc-7* activations of VGG-19 (Simonyan and Zisserman, 2014) and second is *fc-7* activations of Hybrid model (Zhou et al., 2014). VGG-19 is a Convolutional Neural Network (CNN) model trained on ImageNet dataset which consists of 1000 different image classes (Russakovsky et al., 2015), while Hybrid is an CNN architecture that is trained on a combina-

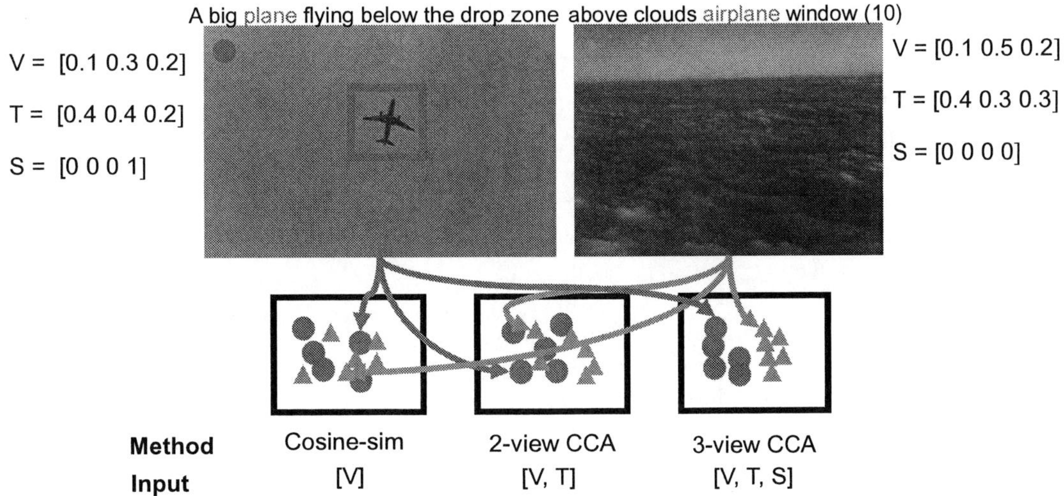

Figure 3: Here, three different embedding spaces are shown. Suppose red circle denotes the image on the left (and all images with aeroplanes visible) and green triangle denotes the image on the right (and all images with aeroplane missing). Nearest neighbor approach takes only visual representation of images V as input, thus these images may be considered similar. Projection gets better for 2-view CCA using $[V, T]$, however since they have similar textual representations, they still lie close in space. For 3-view CCA, with the inclusion of semantic category S, the embedding becomes distinguishable.

tion of Places (Zhou et al., 2014) (a large-scale scene recognition dataset) and ImageNet. Both architectures yield a $4096d$ representation per image. We use cosine-similarity between visual descriptors of each image and retrieve N nearest neighbors (images and their captions) per query. When measuring similarity, we also experimented with Euclidean distance, but found cosine distance to perform better for our purposes. After retrieving N neighbors, denoted as $NN(I_i)$, the candidate object classes for image I_i is the list of all objects in the captions of the neighbors $M_{NN(I_i)}$ that occur more than the mean frequency of the class occurrence counts. Formally, $C_i = \{c_j, c_j \in M_{NN(I_i)}, |c_j| \geq \tau\}$, where $\tau = \frac{1}{N} \sum_{c_j \in M_{NN(I_i)}} |c_j|$.

4.2.2 2-view CCA based estimation

Canonical Correlation Analysis (CCA) embedding (Hardoon et al., 2004) is an excellent tool for modelling data of different modalities, such as images I and their captions T (Hodosh et al., 2013). By using CCA, one can measure similarities (or differences) between different modalities in a common embedding space. Formally, CCA aims to minimize the following objective function:

$$\underset{W_1, W_2}{\text{minimize}} \quad \|(V_{train})W_1 - (L_{train})W_2\|_2^F \quad (1)$$

where W_1 and W_2 are visual and textual projection vectors and V_{train} and L_{train} are visual and textual representations of the training data, respectively. Here, for textual representation of captions, we use Fisher-encoded word2vec features (Klein et al., 2014; Plummer et al., 2015; Mikolov et al., 2013). Each word in a caption is first represented with a 300-D word2vec feature, then encoded within a Fisher Vector framework using 30 clusters. This results in a 18.000-D textual representation of each caption. Before projection, we reduce each modality's dimension to 1000-D for computational efficiency. Then, we learn the projection vectors using training data.

At test stage, we project the visual representation of a test image V_{test} to the common embedding space as $V_{projected} = V_{test}.W_1$ and measure similarity between projections of training images and the test image. Here, we again use the cosine similarity metric between projections. In our experiments, we use normalized-CCA as it yields better performance (Gong et al., 2014b) and normalize projections using corresponding eigenvectors. Similar to nearest-neighbour based candidate object estimation, we again retrieve N training images (and captions $M_{NN_{2CCA}(I_i)}$) on the common embedding space, and use the list of all object classes frequently occurring in the retrieved captions as C_i, *ie.* $C_i = \{c_j, c_j \in M_{NN_{2CCA}(I_i)}, |c_i| \geq \tau\}$.

4.2.3 3-view CCA based estimation

Our final retrieval strategy utilizes 3-view CCA embeddings. 3-view CCA, firstly proposed by (Gong et al., 2014a) is a generalized form of 2-view CCA by including a third view that correlates with the other views. In (Gong et al., 2014a), the authors propose 3-view CCA to achieve multi-modal retrieval between images and tags/keywords associated with images on the web. Third view can be seen as an additional supervision that guides visual and textual projections W_1-W_2 such that semantically related data are more accurately grouped. Formally, 3-view CCA solves the following minimization problem:

$$\underset{W_1, W_2, W_3}{\text{minimize}} \| (V_{train})W_1 - (L_{train})W_2 \|_2^F +$$
$$\| (V_{train})W_1 - (S_{train})W_3 \|_2^F +$$
$$\| (L_{train})W_2 - (S_{train})W_3 \|_2^F +$$

where the first term is equal to the 2-view formulation and third view is induced by second and third terms, using S_{train} and W_3. S_{train} represents our third-view representation for the training set and W_3 is the corresponding projection matrix into embeddding space. Semantically, similar visual and textual representations should be projected to nearby locations and the semantic view S should be aligned with both V and L. For V and L, we use the same setting as in 2-view CCA.

In (Gong et al., 2014a), the authors use keyword or tag-derived textual representations for the third view. In our case, we use two alternatives:

- Class view from captions (denoted as S_T): Each class name is assigned a unique index $i \in [1, 19]$ and then convert it to a 16-bit binary $\in (0, 1)$. For each training image, we assign corresponding binary vector to annotated object's class(es). If more than one object is available, we apply bitwise OR operation to account for each object in the image.

- Visual view from annotated image regions (denoted as S_R): For each annotated object region in an image, we extract visual descriptors. Note that, the first view is extracted from the whole image, whereas this third view alternative uses visual information from individual regions. If there is more than one image annotation, we apply mean pooling.

Both alternatives try to assign images and captions with similar (candidate) objects to lie on close regions in the embedding space. Similar to nearest-neighbor and 2-view CCA, we retrieve N most similar images and corresponding captions for each test image to form the set of candidate object classes.

Figure 3 illustrates an example for the intuition behind using the third view. Suppose there are two images where each caption includes the *aeroplane* class. Although one of the images really shows an image of an aeroplane, the other is captured from an aeroplane window, so no aeroplane is seen. Both their textual representations T include aeroplane, whereas their visual representations V and semantic representations S differ significantly. Using both of these views, these images project into farther points in the embedding space compared to the naive cosine-similarity space and 2-view CCA embeddings, thus can easily be distinguished.

5 Experiments

For experiments, we split our dataset as 50%-50% as training and test. We use Faster R-CNN (Ren et al., 2015) as our base object detector. The detector itself is trained on the PASCAL VOC 2012 data (Everingham et al., 2012). We emply PASCAL (Everingham et al., 2012) conventions while evaluating the methods and also set the set of possible object classes C to Pascal classes (excluding the person class, due to the high level of ambiguity of the captions of this class), so we have 19 classes in total. Following the regular detection experimental settings, we measure intersection-over-union (IoU) between detection and annotation windows and count the detections as positive detections if their IoU exceeds the threshold 0.50%. We evaluate the performance using average precision (AP). While selecting the similar images, the number of nearest images N is assigned to different values of $(10, 20, 50, 100, 150)$.

The first experiments evaluate the performance of Faster R-CNN by running the detector for every object class without considering any textual information, referred as *All classes*. In the second experiment, we assume that we have access to the captions of the test images and run the detector only for the objects mentioned in these captions. This experiment can be interpreted as using an unreliable oracle, since the objects mentioned

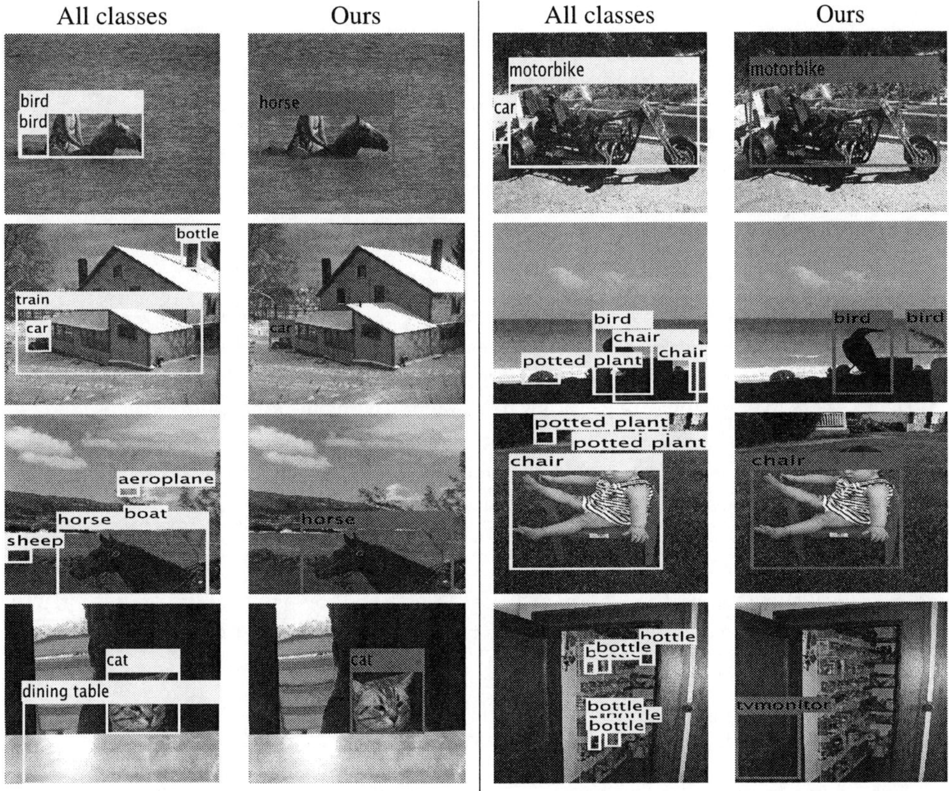

Figure 4: Example detection results illustrating the performance improvements using caption information. The last row shows two failure cases.

in the text do not need to exist in the images as discussed before. We refer to this method as *Mentioned classes*. The quantitative results of these experiments are given in Table 4. As can be seen, based detector results are quite inferior, compared to the case when the list of objects are limited to the set of objects in the given image captions.

The third set of experiments consider a more general setup, where we do not have access to captions of newly seen images, and assess the performance of data-driven estimation of object classes from similar images. In particular, we run the detector for only those candidate object classes that are gathered by retrieving the N closest images and using the frequent object classes mentioned in the retrieved captions. Here, we consider three different approaches. Firstly, we consider only visual similarities of VGG (Simonyan and Zisserman, 2014) and Hybrid (Zhou et al., 2014) activations of the test and training images as described in Sec.4.2.1. In the second and third approaches, we use the embedding spaces learned via the 2-view and 3-view CCA as introduced in Sec.4.2.2

and Sec.4.2.3, respectively.

Table 2 shows the results of our object detection schemes which consider data-driven approaches to limit the object detectors. In general, we observe that VGG activations as deep features yield better results than HYBRID activations. As the number of closest images increase, we are able to predict the candidate object classes more accurately, and obtain better performances for all retrieval scenarios. In general, 3-view CCA gives the best results over the other alternatives.

In Table 3, we show the object detection results for different choices of the third view for 3-way CCA. As demonstrated, the region-based deep activations result in a better embedding space than the binary class vectors, providing more accurate object detection results.

Finally, we compare the results of all of our experiments. As can be seen in Table 4 and Figure 4, Faster R-CNN produces many false positive when run with all the object classes. When it is run with the classes mentioned in the given caption, the accuracy improves as expected. Interestingly,

Table 2: Mean Average precision (mAP) values for detection through data-driven estimation of object classes. Each approach is tested by retrieving $N = (10, 20, 50, 100, 150)$ similar images. For 3-view CCA, the binary class (S_T) is used as the third view.

Deep image feature	Method	10	20	50	100	150
	Single view	0.385	0.428	0.473	0.495	0.504
Hybrid	2-view CCA	0.396	0.421	0.480	0.492	0.504
	3-view CCA	0.399	0.425	**0.487**	0.501	0.499
	Single view	0.403	0.432	0.479	0.492	0.499
VGG	2-view CCA	0.413	0.443	0.484	**0.511**	0.512
	3-view CCA	**0.416**	**0.451**	0.486	0.508	**0.515**

Table 3: Mean Average precision (mAP) values for detection using the embedding spaces learned through 3-view CCA using binary class vectors (S_T) or deep visual feature averaged over annotated object regions (S_R) as the third views. V and S represents our first and third view choices respectively.

V	S	Method	10	20	50	100	150
Hybrid	Binary class (S_T)	3-view CCA	0.399	0.425	0.487	0.501	0.499
	Region features (S_R)	3-view CCA	0.418	**0.455**	0.496	**0.511**	0.517
VGG	Binary class (S_T)	3-view CCA	0.416	0.451	0.486	0.508	0.515
	Region features (S_R)	3-view CCA	**0.419**	0.448	**0.503**	0.508	**0.518**

Table 4: Mean Average precision (mAP) values of the Faster R-CNN run with all classes, classes mentioned in the captions and the predicted candidate object classes.

			Predicted classes		
Method	All classes	Mentioned classes	Single view	2-view CCA	3-view CCA
AP	0.304	0.508	0.504	0.512	**0.518**

our multi-view prediction approaches give highly competitive and even better results than using the captions of the test images.

6 Conclusion

In this paper, we develop methods to improve performance of object detection using captions in the wild. Captions are freely available textual image descriptions written by the users, exhibiting a high range of challenges due to excessive noise. To overcome these limitations, we develop data-driven methods that can achieve better performance than the current state-of-the-art object detector Faster R-CNN by means of estimating likely objects in the images. We compare different strategies that use different levels of supervision. We show that superior results can be obtained even without access to image's *own* caption, by leveraging (somewhat noisy) captions of similar images. The results clearly indicate that captions are beneficial supervisory signals for object detection problem, when used in a data-driven manner.

In the future, we plan to extend our dataset using larger-scale image-caption pairs datasets such as Flickr-100M (Thomee et al., 2016). We also plan to apply similar ideas to co-localization problem (Tang et al., 2014) where noisy images can also be determined by data-driven methods.

7 Acknowledgements

This research was supported in part by The Scientific and Technological Research Council of Turkey (TUBITAK), Career Development Award 113E116.

References

T. L. Berg, A. C. Berg, J. Edwards, M. Maire, R. White, Yee-Whye Teh, E. Learned-Miller, and D. A. Forsyth. 2004. Names and faces in the news. In *CVPR 2004. Proceedings of the 2004 IEEE Computer Society Conference on*, volume 2, pages II–848–II–854 Vol.2.

A. C. Berg, T. L. Berg, H. Daum, J. Dodge, A. Goyal, X. Han, A. Mensch, M. Mitchell, A. Sood,

K. Stratos, and K. Yamaguchi. 2012. Understanding and predicting importance in images. In *CVPR*, pages 3562–3569.

T. Chen, Dongyuan Lu, Min-Yen Kan, and Peng Cui. 2013. Understanding and classifying image tweets. In *Proceedings of the 21st ACM international conference on Multimedia*, pages 781–784. ACM.

J. Chen, Polina Kuznetsova, David Warren, and Yejin Choi. 2015. Déja image-captions: A corpus of expressive descriptions in repetition. In *Proceedings of the 2015 NAACL: Human Language Technologies*, pages 504–514.

Ming-Ming Cheng, Shuai Zheng, Wen-Yan Lin, Vibhav Vineet, Paul Sturgess, Nigel Crook, Niloy J. Mitra, and Philip Torr. 2014. Imagespirit: Verbal guided image parsing. *ACM Trans. Graph.*, 34(1):3:1–3:11, December.

R. G. Cinbis, J. Verbeek, and C. Schmid. 2016. Weakly supervised object localization with multifold multiple instance learning. *Pattern Analysis and Machine Intelligence, IEEE Transactions on*, pages 1–1.

J. Dodge, Amit Goyal, Xufeng Han, Alyssa Mensch, Margaret Mitchell, Karl Stratos, Kota Yamaguchi, Yejin Choi, Hal Daumé III, Alexander C Berg, et al. 2012. Detecting visual text. In *Proceedings of the 2012 NAACL: Human Language Technologies*, pages 762–772. Association for Computational Linguistics.

M. Everingham, J. Sivic, and A. Zisserman. 2009. Taking the bite out of automatic naming of characters in TV video. *Image and Vision Computing*, 27(5).

M. Everingham, L. Van Gool, C. K. I. Williams, J. Winn, and A. Zisserman. 2012. The PASCAL Visual Object Classes Challenge 2012 (VOC2012) Results. http://www.pascal-network.org.

A. Farhadi, Mohsen Hejrati, Mohammad Amin Sadeghi, Peter Young, Cyrus Rashtchian, Julia Hockenmaier, and David Forsyth. 2010. Every picture tells a story: Generating sentences from images. In *Computer Vision–ECCV 2010*, pages 15–29. Springer.

S. Fidler, A. Sharma, and R. Urtasun. 2013. A sentence is worth a thousand pixels. In *CVPR, 2013 IEEE Conference on*, pages 1995–2002.

Y. Gong, Qifa Ke, Michael Isard, and Svetlana Lazebnik. 2014a. A multi-view embedding space for modeling internet images, tags, and their semantics. *IJCV*, 106(2):210–233.

Y. Gong, Liwei Wang, Micah Hodosh, Julia Hockenmaier, and Svetlana Lazebnik. 2014b. Improving image-sentence embeddings using large weakly annotated photo collections. In *Computer Vision–ECCV 2014*, pages 529–545. Springer.

D. R. Hardoon, Sandor Szedmak, and John Shawe-Taylor. 2004. Canonical correlation analysis: An overview with application to learning methods. *Neural computation*, 16(12):2639–2664.

M. Hodosh, Peter Young, Cyrus Rashtchian, and Julia Hockenmaier. 2010. Cross-caption coreference resolution for automatic image understanding. In *Proceedings of the Fourteenth Conference on CoNLL 2010, Uppsala, Sweden, July 15-16, 2010*, pages 162–171.

M. Hodosh, Peter Young, and Julia Hockenmaier. 2013. Framing Image Description as a Ranking Task: Data, Models and Evaluation Metrics. *JAIR*, 47:853–899.

F. Keller, Desmond Elliott, et al. 2014. Visual and linguistic treebank.

B. Klein, Guy Lev, Gil Sadeh, and Lior Wolf. 2014. Fisher vectors derived from hybrid gaussian-laplacian mixture models for image annotation. *arXiv preprint arXiv:1411.7399*.

C. Kong, D. Lin, M. Bansal, R. Urtasun, and S. Fidler. 2014. What are you talking about? text-to-image coreference. In *2014 IEEE CVPR*, pages 3558–3565.

Y. LeCun, Yoshua Bengio, and Geoffrey Hinton. 2015. Deep learning. *Nature*, 521(7553):436–444.

Tsung-Yi Lin, Michael Maire, Serge Belongie, James Hays, Pietro Perona, Deva Ramanan, Piotr Dollár, and C Lawrence Zitnick. 2014. Microsoft COCO: Common objects in context. In *ECCV*.

T. Mikolov, Kai Chen, Greg Corrado, and Jeffrey Dean. 2013. Efficient estimation of word representations in vector space. *arXiv preprint arXiv:1301.3781*.

V. Ordonez, Xufeng Han, Polina Kuznetsova, Girish Kulkarni, Margaret Mitchell, Kota Yamaguchi, Karl Stratos, Amit Goyal, Jesse Dodge, Alyssa Mensch, et al. 2015. Large scale retrieval and generation of image descriptions. *IJCV*, pages 1–14.

M. Pandey and S. Lazebnik. 2011. Scene recognition and weakly supervised object localization with deformable part-based models. In *2011 ICCV*, pages 1307–1314.

B. A Plummer, Liwei Wang, Chris M Cervantes, Juan C Caicedo, Julia Hockenmaier, and Svetlana Lazebnik. 2015. Flickr30k entities: Collecting region-to-phrase correspondences for richer image-to-sentence models. In *Proceedings of the IEEE ICCV*, pages 2641–2649.

B. Raffaella, R. Cakici, D. Elliott, A. Erdem, E. Erdem, N. Ikizler-Cinbis, F. Keller, A. Muscat, and B. Plank. 2016. Automatic description generation from images: A survey of models, datasets, and evaluation measures. *JAIR*, 55:409–442.

C. Rashtchian, Peter Young, Micah Hodosh, and Julia Hockenmaier. 2010a. Collecting image annotations using amazon's mechanical turk. In *NAACL: Human Language Technologies Workshop on Creating Speech and Language Data with Amazon's Mechanical Turk*.

C. Rashtchian, Peter Young, Micah Hodosh, and Julia Hockenmaier. 2010b. Collecting image annotations using amazon's mechanical turk. In *Proceedings of the NAACL HLT 2010 Workshop on Creating Speech and Language Data with Amazon's Mechanical Turk*, pages 139–147. Association for Computational Linguistics.

S. Ren, Kaiming He, Ross Girshick, and Jian Sun. 2015. Faster r-cnn: Towards real-time object detection with region proposal networks. In *Advances in Neural Information Processing Systems*, pages 91–99.

A. Rohrbach, Marcus Rohrbach, Ronghang Hu, Trevor Darrell, and Bernt Schiele. 2015. Grounding of textual phrases in images by reconstruction. *arXiv:1511.03745*.

O. Russakovsky, Jia Deng, Hao Su, Jonathan Krause, Sanjeev Satheesh, Sean Ma, Zhiheng Huang, Andrej Karpathy, Aditya Khosla, Michael Bernstein, et al. 2015. Imagenet large scale visual recognition challenge. *IJCV*, 115(3):211–252.

K. Simonyan and Andrew Zisserman. 2014. Very deep convolutional networks for large-scale image recognition. *arXiv preprint arXiv:1409.1556*.

P. Siva and Tao Xiang. 2011. Weakly supervised object detector learning with model drift detection. In *2011 ICCV*, pages 343–350.

K. Tang, Armand Joulin, Li-Jia Li, and Li Fei-Fei. 2014. Co-localization in real-world images. In *Computer Vision and Pattern Recognition (CVPR), 2014 IEEE Conference on*, pages 1464–1471. IEEE.

B. Thomee, David A Shamma, Gerald Friedland, Benjamin Elizalde, Karl Ni, Douglas Poland, Damian Borth, and Li-Jia Li. 2016. Yfcc100m: The new data in multimedia research. *Communications of the ACM*, 59(2):64–73.

J. Xu, A. G. Schwing, and R. Urtasun. 2014. Tell me what you see and i will show you where it is. In *2014 IEEE CVPR*.

M. Yatskar, Michel Galley, Lucy Vanderwende, and Luke Zettlemoyer. 2014. See no evil, say no evil: Description generation from densely labeled images. In *Third Joint Conference on Lexical and Computation Semantics (*SEM)*.

P. Young, Alice Lai, Micah Hodosh, and Julia Hockenmaier. 2014a. From image descriptions to visual denotations: New similarity metrics for semantic inference over event descriptions. *Transactions of the ACL*, 2:67–78.

P. Young, Alice Lai, Micah Hodosh, and Julia Hockenmaier. 2014b. From image descriptions to visual denotations: New similarity metrics for semantic inference over event descriptions. *Transactions of the ACL*, 2:67–78.

B. Zhou, Agata Lapedriza, Jianxiong Xiao, Antonio Torralba, and Aude Oliva. 2014. Learning deep features for scene recognition using places database. In *NIPS*, pages 487–495.

Natural Language Descriptions of Human Activities Scenes: Corpus Generation and Analysis

Nouf Al Harbi

Department of Computer Science, University of Sheffield, Sheffield, United Kingdom
Department of Computer Science and Engineering, Taibah University, Medina, Saudi Arabia
`nmalharbi1@sheffield.ac.uk`

Yoshihiko Gotoh

Department of Computer Science, University of Sheffield, Sheffield, United Kingdom
`y.gotoh@sheffield.ac.uk`

Abstract

There has been continuous growth in the volume and ubiquity of video material. It has become essential to define video semantics in order to aid the searchability and retrieval of this data. Although the method of annotating this data with keywords is relatively well researched, the quality can be improved through describing videos with natural language. We are exploring approaches to generating natural language descriptions of inter-relations between human activities in a video stream. This paper focuses on creation of a dataset that can be used for development and evaluation. To this end a corpus of video clips, manually selected from the Hollywood2 dataset, and their natural language descriptions has been generated. Analysis of the hand annotation presents insights into human interests and thoughts. Such resource can be used to evaluate automatic natural language generation systems for video.

1 Introduction

Video synopses can be created by converting video summaries using natural language. They serve to generate a multimedia archive where video analysis, retrieval and summarisation can be developed. The majority of previous research, in particular for video description tasks, has relied upon short video clips. They typically presented one subject performing one action, hence a single sentence was often sufficient to annotate them. By contrast reality-based video scenarios incorporate various camera shots depicting a range of actions.

We are exploring approaches to generating natural language description for inter-relations of hu-mans and their activities within video streams. The first step of the study was to create a dataset that could be used for development and evaluation, as we did not find publicly available resource that suitably considered the spatial and temporal relations between individual entities. Initially, from the Human Actions and Scenes dataset (Hollywood2 dataset[1]), 120 video segments were selected, 10 for each of the twelve categories. They were relatively long videos ranging from 1 to 3 minutes, selected based on a number of criteria, such as the number of camera shots and the variety of human actions. For selected video clips, a dataset was then created, comprising hand annotations with natural language descriptions. We refer to this dataset as NLDHA[2] Corpus.

The contributions of the work presented in this paper include the following two aspects:

- A total of 12 participants manually annotated this dataset in two ways: a brief synopsis (title) consisting of a single phrase or sentence, and a full explanation in everyday language, set out using a number of sentences.

- An action classification experiment based on hand annotations was performed to demonstrate the application of the corpus with natural language descriptions.

2 Related Work

There are a variety of corpora in the video processing studies, ranging from basic object recognition to analysis of complex scenes. Unfortunately most video corpora for visual event recognition are not suitable for evaluating their natural language description. For example the KTH dataset (Schuldt

---

[1] www.di.ens.fr/~laptev/actions/hollywood2

[2] 'NLDHA' stands for Natural Language Descriptions for Human Activities in videos.

39

Proceedings of the 5th Workshop on Vision and Language, pages 39–47,
Berlin, Germany, August 12 2016. ©2016 Association for Computational Linguistics

et al., 2004) and the Weizmann dataset (Blank et al., 2005) facilitate depicting events with a single human, thus there is no interaction with other individuals or objects. Recently a number of video corpora have been created, aiming at annotation with natural language. They are designed with certain prerequisites or constraints to fulfil the specific task or the purpose. Some of these corpora are reviewed in the following.

ACL2013 dataset[3]. A methodology was proposed by (Yu and Siskind, 2013) to learn word meanings from video that was coupled with sentences. A range of combined situations could be compiled into a dataset of 61 short filmed video clips, each with 3-5 seconds and 640×480 resolution at 40 fps (frames per second). Every clip was made up of a combination of a number of synchronous instances, which could involve a subset of up to four different entities: a chair, a garbage can, a backpack and a person. The corpus of 159 training examples coupled up videos with more than one sentence and sentences with more than one video — on average there were 2.6 sentences per video. Some of these video clips depicted non-human objects' activities without human presence, such as an airplane landing, which makes this dataset not suitable for our task.

TACoS Cooking dataset[4]. This dataset was created for addressing the issue of grounding sentences to describe actions in visual information extracted from videos (Regneri et al., 2013). 127 videos with 26 basic cooking tasks were included and 22 subjects were used for recording a corpus in the kitchen environment. 20 different textual descriptions were collected for each video, resulting in 2540 annotation assignments. This corpus was designed for the specific purpose of cooking and, as a result, all actions were centred on the kitchen environment, which makes it not suitable for a general video description task.

SumMe dataset[5]. SumMe was a new benchmark proposed for the task of summarizing video (Gygli et al., 2014). There were in total 25 videos included in the SumMe dataset, covering sports, events and holidays. The video length varied between 1 and 6 minutes. The study included a total of 41 participants (19 males and 22 females) that had different educational backgrounds, for summarizing the videos' visual content. Around 15 to 18 people summarised each video. Since there is no human present in some videos, this dataset is inappropriate for our task.

3 Corpus Generation

We have created the NLDHA Corpus of English language, describing 12 action classes from real-life video scenes, observed in the manually selected subset of the Hollywood2 dataset which was collected from 69 Hollywood films. This dataset was selected as it had realistic and generic video settings including human subjects with various activities, emotions and interactions with others. We have selected 10 video clips for each of 12 action classes, resulting in 120 video clips in total. The selected clips contained either (1) multiple camera shots of human activities to incorporate temporal and spatial association of human activities, or (2) a single shot consisting of a variety of actions, performed either by one or multiple persons. The intention was to develop a compact dataset to study approaches for translating video contents of human interaction and their temporal and spatial relations to natural language descriptions. For each of 120 video clips, NLDHA consists of 12 descriptions obtained via Amazon Mechanical Turk (MTurk)[6].

The majority of selected segments contained multiple camera shots, with 6 shots on average, varying between indoor and outdoor scene-settings. The total length of the selected clips was 225,000 frames, with a frame rate of 25 fps and the average length of 1875 frames for each video. Videos span between 1 and 3 minutes, with the average length of 75 seconds. Human interactions may be classified into two themes:

human-human interaction: This involves multiple humans, including categories such as 'FightPerson', 'HandShake', 'HugPerson', 'SitUp', 'Run' and 'Kiss'.

human-object interaction: A human performes some action with an object (*e.g.*, car, chair or dining table), such as '*driving*', '*sitting*' or '*eating*'. This includes the following categories: 'AnswerPhone', 'DriveCar', 'SitDown', 'StandUp', 'Eat' and 'GetOutCar'.

All categories involved human activities, expressions and emotions. A sequence of actions was

---

[3]haonanyu.com/research/acl2013
[4]www.coli.uni-saarland.de/projects/smile/page.php?id=tacos
[5]www.vision.ee.ethz.ch/gyglim/vsum

[6]www.mturk.com

performed by one person, depicted in one shot, whereas multiple shots presented relation and interaction between multiple humans. Some videos depicted humans' interaction with other objects in a variety of indoor and outdoor settings.

3.1 Collecting Textual Video Descriptions

Amazon Mechanical Turk (MTurk) was used to collect video descriptions. A Human Intelligence Task (HIT) was created and published on MTurk, using an adapted version of the annotation tool Vatic (Vondrick et al., 2013). For each video we collected 12 different textual annotations, leading to 1440 annotation assignments. Each annotator prepared manual descriptions for 120 video segments in two different types: title assignment (a single phrase) and full description (multiple sentences). A title, in some sense, can be considered as a summary provided in the most compact form, which includes the essential themes, or contents of a video in a short phrase. In contrast, full description is detailed and comprises of a number of sentences with in-depth description of objects, their activities and interactions. In the rest of this paper they are referred to as 'hand annotation'. A valuable resource for text-based video retrieval and summarisation can be created through the combination of titles and full descriptions.

For each assignment one video was shown to the annotator, who was then requested to provide a title for the video in one phrase, highlighting the main theme and explaining human activities observed in the video. The annotator was also asked to provide a description of minimum 5 and maximum 15 complete English sentences for explaining the events in the video. In order to help annotators understand the task, they were presented with a sample video segment, as well as possible textual annotations, *i.e.*, a title and a complete description. Instructions were provided, allowing an open vocabulary, meaning that annotators had the freedom to use any English word. However annotators were asked not to use (1) computer codes or symbols, (2) proper nouns (*e.g.*, person's name), and (3) information identified through audio, since they could affect the quality of descriptions for semantic video content.

4 Corpus Analysis

With 12 annotators describing each of 120 videos, there are 1440 documents in this corpus. The to-

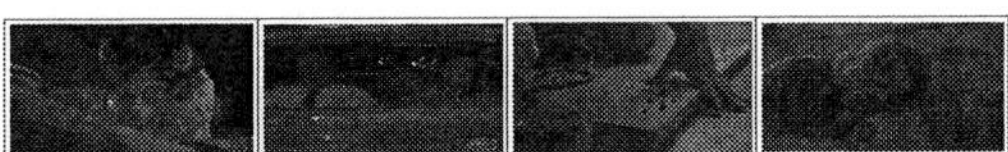

Hand annotation 1
(**title**) Furious man crushing a window on the car;
(**description**) Furious man is crushing window on the car with iron stick and screaming; After that, we see him and the other two men driving in the car; All except the driver are eating sandwiches; Then we see driver sticking nails in wooden lath;

Hand annotation 2
(**title**) Beating a car and running;
(**description**) Angry man begins beating up a car; He breaks the windshield and windows; Then there are three men riding in another car; They are eating and riding somewhere; Then a man is beating nails into a board;

Hand annotation 3
(**title**) Smashing a car window;
(**description**) A man is smashing the window of a parked car with a sledge hammer at night; Next, the man who was speaking on the phone is driving a car with two other men as passengers at night; Later, another man is speaking on the phone while hammering nails in a board;

Hand annotation 4
(**title**) Broken windshield of a car;
(**description**) A man breaks the front windshield of a car using a rod; Then the same car is driven by three men; Later, one among them makes a call inside the car;

Hand annotation 5
(**title**) A windshieldless car driving;
(**description**) A man smashing in a windshield with a bat and later three men go for a drive in the car;

Hand annotation 6
(**title**) Car wrecking;
(**description**) A man wrecks a car and then people drive in it;

Figure 1: A montage of a 3-minute video segment and six sets of the hand annotations. This clip was extracted from the 'DriveCar' category in the Hollywood2 dataset, 'actionclipautoautotrain00094', depicting a sequence of actions performed by four humans in an outdoor scene.

tal number of words is 67080, hence the average length of one document is roughly 47 words. There are 5136 unique words and 2336 keywords consisting of nouns and verbs. Figure 1 presents six annotation examples for one of video clips from the 'DriveCar' category. This video segment consisted of four different shots depicting multiple actions performed by four humans, with the two main activities, '*smashing*' and '*driving*'.

The hand annotations have been made in two types: 'title' and 'description'. A title often consists of only a couple of words that do not constitute a complete sentence. Verbs are often used to express the main theme of the video, *e.g.*, '*family eating dinner*', '*men fighting*' and '*three people driving*'. The average length of titles is three words. An extensive analysis on titles indicates that, for each video, the same theme was identified by most annotators, though there were differences between them in the words used to express the theme. Figure 1 clearly illustrates that six

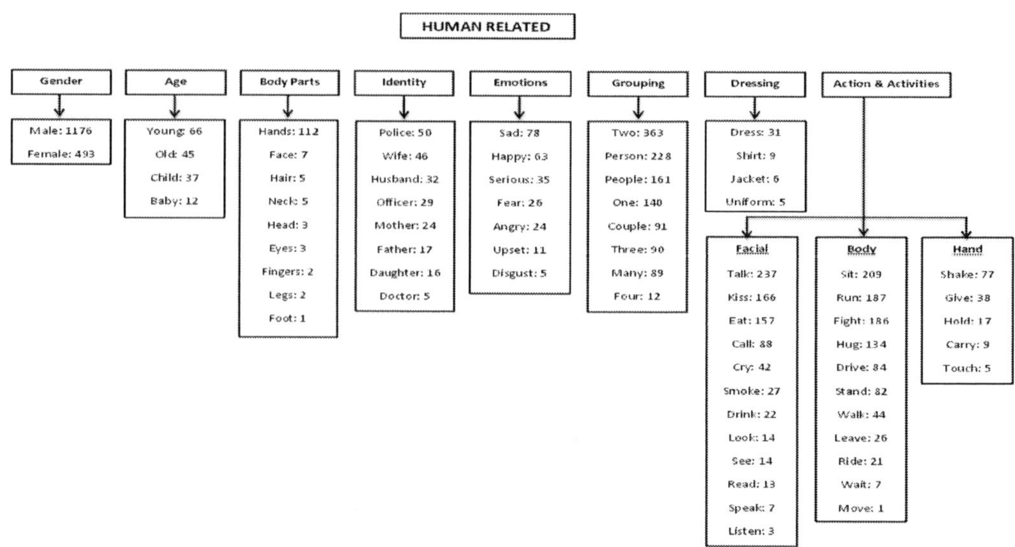

Figure 2: Human related features and their occurrences found in the hand annotations.

annotators were expressing the same theme using different words — 'crushing', 'beat up', 'smash', 'break' and 'wreck'.

On the other hand, full descriptions on average contain four to six phrases or sentences; typically each camera shot is described by one sentence. Most sentences are concise, ranging between six and eight words. Descriptions for human, gender, emotion and actions, with their temporal order, are commonly observed. Minor details for objects, dressing and location are only occasionally stated, unless these objects participate in the event. Annotations vary in a wide range from highly abstract to very detailed descriptions, although they typically preserved the temporal order of activities performed in the video clip. The amount of detail included in full descriptions can be observed in examples presented in Figure 1. They vary between the very compact (*e.g.*, annotation 6), to the very detailed (*e.g.*, annotation 3). Nevertheless almost all annotations maintain the same temporal order of activities performed in the video.

4.1 Human Related Features

Figure 2 illustrates the human-related information that is highlighted in the hand annotations. Full attention was paid to the human presence in the video by the annotators, in particular gender specification for female and male are most frequently observed. Note that in the '*female*' category, related words indicating female, such as '*lady*' and 'woman' are also included; and so are in the 'male' category. This supports that humans and their attributes which identify as high level visual features (HLFs) are the most important and interesting information for annotators. By contrast some factors such as identity (*e.g.*, '*police officer*', '*father*') and age information (*e.g.*, '*young*', '*old*', '*child*') are not observed very often. Human body parts have mixed occurrences, ranging from high ('*hand*') to low ('*foot*').

Six basic emotions were presented in (Ekman, 1992); they relate to the most frequent facial expressions, including fear, anger, sadness, surprise, disgust and happiness. Another interesting feature is dressing; when an individual has dressed in a unique manner, for instance wearing a formal suit, an army, a police uniform or a coloured jacket, it was described; otherwise dressing information was not stated frequently. Scenes with multiple humans were also very common, and therefore, grouping information were frequently stated. Human activities were identified through the involvement of body parts, including actions such as '*walking*', '*running*', '*sitting*', '*fighting*' and '*standing*'. It was also observed among the majority of annotators that they liked to describe using general terms (*e.g.*, '*female*') rather than their specific identities (*e.g.*, '*doctor*').

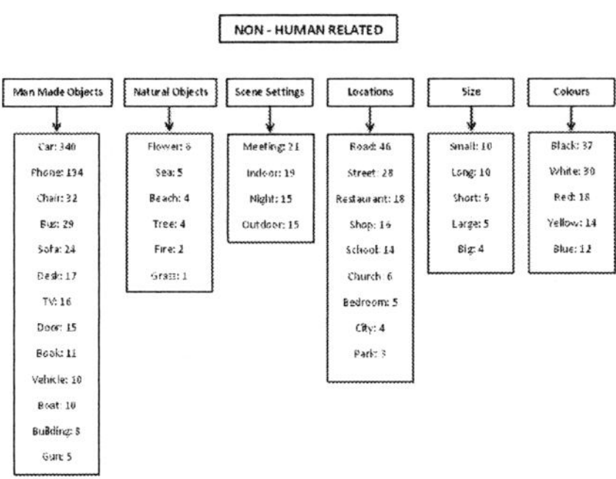

Figure 3: Non-human features and their occurrences in the hand annotations.

4.2 Objects and Scene Settings

Figure 3 illustrates the hierarchy of visual features that are not found in Figure 2. Many of them denote artificial objects, and interaction between humans and these objects are stated to complete activities, *e.g.*, 'man is sitting on chair', 'he is driving a car' and 'she is talking on the phone'. Other important information is location (*e.g.*, 'restaurant', 'shop', 'school'), which identifies object's position in the scene (*e.g.*, 'people are eating in the restaurant', 'there is a car on the road').

When identifying individual high level features (HLFs), colour information often plays an essential role — *e.g.*, 'she is wearing a white uniform', 'a man in a black shirt is walking with a woman with a green jacket'. Considering the great number of colour occurrences, it is evident that humans have an interest in observing the colour scheme in visual scenes, along with the objects. We are able to observe individual annotators' interest in foreground/background. Some annotators also paid attention to outdoor/indoor scene settings. Details for prominent objects in a visual scene was demonstrated by some annotations — *e.g.*, 'two boys are seated on a small boat', 'a lady with long hair is walking on the road'. Natural objects were rarely described in the hand annotations.

4.3 Spatial Relations

Visual scenes in filming are best described in terms of spatial relations, which can define how objects are located spatially in relation to some reference object. In a video stream this reference object is usually in the foreground. The competent

in: 653; on: 335; with: 235; at: 121; between: 36; around: 26; behind: 25; touch: 23; middle: 21; together: 20; inside: 17; far: 16; in front of: 13; beside: 11; on the right: 10; on the left: 8; near: 6; under: 5; in the middle: 3

Figure 4: List of frequent spatial relations and their frequency counts, manually collated from the hand annotations.

use of prepositions, such as *on, at, inside* or *above*, can facilitate the creation of smooth and concise descriptions when presenting the spatial relations between objects. For example 'three people are swimming in the canal' provides more descriptive detail than 'three people are swimming' and 'there is a canal in the background' separately. There are a variety of expressions that can be used to gain accurate spatial representations, *e.g.*, direction ('left', 'under'), distance ('far', 'near'), or topology ('touch', 'inside') (Cohn et al., 2008).

A list of the most frequent words in the corpus concerning spatial relations are presented in Figure 4. Frequent occurrences of these words indicate people's regular use when describing visual scenes. Semantics of the visual scenes are better understood through the use of these words with which we are able to identify connections between various HLFs. For various reasons they had to be manually counted. Firstly, some words in the list may have a multitude of alternative uses in addition to spatial relations. The following three phrases demonstrate how the word 'in' can be used for different purposes: 'three people are sitting in a car' represents a spatial relation, whilst 'the dog in the last shot' depicts a relationship between various scenes, and 'two people in a dialogue' augments the ease with which the description can be read. Secondly, the spatial word can be a preposition by itself; *e.g.*, 'in' or syntactically overlapped with another preposition such as 'three persons are talking in front of shops at night'. Finally, there are some preposition words that can be used for both spatial and temporal relations; *e.g.*, 'at' in the following example, 'a man is smashing the window of a parked car with a sledge hammer at night' presents the temporal relation, whereas 'at' in 'there are three people eating dinner at home' indicates the spatial relation.

4.4 Temporal Relations

When something happens, temporal expressions, such as *before, long, awhile* or *during*, describe

Single human
then: 125; after: 60; afterwards: 44; before: 42; later on: 32; throughout: 32; start: 27; end: 25; next: 25; finish: 25;

Multiple humans
while: 87; meeting:71; during: 27; overlap: 12; meanwhile: 12; throughout: 12; then: 11; equals: 4,

Figure 5: List of frequent temporal relations and their frequency counts in the NLDHA Corpus.

the duration or how often it occurs (Pustejovsky et al., 2003). Temporal and spatial relations are combined in videos as time series data using highly sophisticated multi-dimensional contents. A complete video sequence is created by linking individual scenes. Annotators use temporal relations to combine the narratives for a sequence of scenes and produce a complete account of the video content. In the following example, three separate scenes can be connected using two temporal relations, *then* and *later*:

> 'A man and woman are talking and the woman walks out of the house; **then** she sees him through the door as he is passing in the street; **later**, another man enters the house.'

A total of thirteen relations (*overlaps, overlapped-by, starts, started-by, meets, meet-by, finishes, finished-by, equals, after, before, contains* and *during*) make up a temporal logic, as identified in (Allen and Ferguson, 1994), who also proposed that scenarios could be more often described using time intervals than time points. Analysis of the NLDHA Corpus indicates that temporal relations can be classified into two types: activities of a single human and multiple humans interacting with each other. Figure 5 presents a list of the most frequent temporal relations found in the hand annotations. Clearly keywords, connecting numerous human activities, are important. According to Allen's algebra (Allen and Ferguson, 1994), '*meet*' and '*met by*' are keywords, indicating important temporal relations. This kind of relation occurs frequently in meeting scenes where there are multiple humans present, thus a specific action is performed once another action is completed. '*While*' is also a commonly used temporal keyword as it describes actions carried out simultaneously, *e.g.*, 'a man is eating while his friend is drinking'.

Our observation indicates that, for activities by a single human, temporal relations are typically used in the chronological order of actions, *e.g.*, 'a man comes into the room a little awkwardly; then he sits on the chair'. On the other hand, for the multiple humans scenes, corpus analysis shows that the annotators were likely to pay much more attention to the actions carried out simultaneously by different people, rather than describing individual human activities. Some of video scenes incorporated both types, thus their occurrences had to be counted manually.

4.5 Similarity between Descriptions

Cohen's kappa coefficient (κ) is widely used for calculating the inter-annotator agreement (Cohen, 1960). However, for measuring the similarity in the NLDHA Corpus, a kappa coefficient may not be suitable because of the large variation in the description length among individual annotators. For such situation, a so-called cosine similarity may be more effective because it works independent of document lengths as one of its important properties. The similarity between two documents can be quantified as the cosine of the angle between the vectors when the documents are represented as term vectors.

Let $D = d_1, \ldots, d_n$ denote a set of documents and $T = t_1, \ldots, t_m$ be a set of distinct terms occurring in D. A document is then represented as an m-dimensional vector $\vec{t_d}$. Let $tf(d, t)$ stand for the frequency of term $t \in T$ in document $d \in D$. Then the vector representation of a document d is given by

$$\vec{t_d} = (tf(d, t_1), \ldots, tf(d, t_m)) \tag{1}$$

and the cosine similarity is defined by

$$SIM_C(\vec{t_a}, \vec{t_b}) = \frac{\vec{t_a} \cdot \vec{t_b}}{|\vec{t_a}| \times |\vec{t_b}|} \tag{2}$$

where $\vec{t_a}$ and $\vec{t_b}$ are m-dimensional vectors over the term set $T = t_1, \ldots, t_m$. The numerator represents the dot product of two vectors, while the denominator is the product of their Euclidean lengths. Each dimension is used for representing a term with its weight in the document which is non-negative, due to which the cosine similarity is non-negative and bounded between $[0, 1]$. It is 0 where two documents are totally different, and 1 where they are identical.

To evaluate the similarity between hand annotations, a number of standard text processing filtering techniques are applied. The first is the removal of stop words (Flood, 1999), which are non-descriptive for the purpose of these documents.

The second measure involves stemming, which is reducing words into their base forms using the Porter stemmer (Porter, 1980). Finally it is usually helpful to minimise the vocabulary by substituting words with their common synonyms without affecting meaning, which can be achieved by using the NLTK WordNet interface[7]. Synonyms will reduce the annotators' variation and subjectivity caused by their use of different words for the same concept, and will also increase the occurrence of significant collocations.

The average similarity scores within 12 hand annotations for each of 120 video across 12 categories are shown in Table 1. Individual description scores were used for calculating the average, which was compared with the remaining descriptions in the same category. They were calculated in three conditions: (A) raw hand annotations, (B) applying Porter Stemmer and removing stop words, without replacing synonyms, and (C) without removing stop words, but applying Porter Stemmer and replacing synonyms. The table indicates that condition (C) resulted in the better similarity. In other words, the similarity has increased by replacing some words with their synonyms, indicating that we are expressing the same concept using different terms.

Table 1 also shows that the similarity scores for 'DriveCar', 'AnswerPhone' and 'Eat' categories were higher than the rest. Each of these three categories appeared to have some common factors among hand annotations, resulting from existence of important objects associated with humans and their actions, such as a car, a phone, and a dining table. Most annotators paid attention to such objects, hence common concepts were used for their description, leading to higher similarity scores than others. Conversely for the rest of categories, a broader range of concepts were incorporated in their hand annotations, although they still maintained the similarity by focusing on the same actions (thus using the same verbs).

5   Video Classification Experiments

This section uses an action classification task for demonstrating the application of the NLDHA Corpus with natural language descriptions.

	(A)	(B)	(C)	Average
AnswerPhone	0.5294	0.5236	0.5446	0.5325
DriveCar	0.5564	0.5587	0.5632	0.5594
Eat	0.5272	0.5386	0.5386	0.5348
FightPerson	0.4010	0.4104	0.4245	0.4119
GetOutCar	0.4679	0.4607	0.4707	0.4664
HandShake	0.3955	0.4034	0.4187	0.4058
HugPerson	0.4036	0.4216	0.4236	0.4162
Kiss	0.3868	0.4065	0.4187	0.404
Run	0.3996	0.4056	0.4076	0.4042
SitDown	0.3925	0.4065	0.4158	0.4049
SitUp	0.3898	0.3952	0.4023	0.3958
StandUp	0.4043	0.4074	0.4274	0.4130

Table 1: Similarity scores within 12 hand annotations using the cosine similarity. For each class, scores are calculated in three conditions: (A) raw hand annotations; (B) applying Porter Stemmer and removing stop words, without replacing synonyms; (C) without removing stop words, but applying Porter Stemmer and replacing synonyms.

5.1   Experimental Setup

Textual document features can be expressed through *tf-idf* scores (Dumais et al., 1998). The importance of a term t within a particular document d can be measured by

$$tfidf(t,d) = tf(t,d) \cdot idf(d) \qquad (3)$$

The term frequency $tf(t,d)$ is given by

$$tf(t,d) = \frac{N_{t,d}}{\sum_k N_{k,d}} \qquad (4)$$

where the number of occurrences of t in d is presented by $N_{t,d}$, while the denominator is the size of the document $|d|$. Further, the inverse document frequency $idf(d)$ is

$$idf(d) = \log \frac{N}{W(t)} \qquad (5)$$

where N is the total number of documents in the corpus and $W(t)$ is the total number of documents containing the term t. A term-document matrix is presented by $T \times D$ matrix $\{tfidf(t,d)\}$.

When conducting the experiment, stop words were removed and stemming was applied. For the action classication task, the most frequent 1000 words were used. We applied the Naive Bayes probabilistic supervised learning algorithm from the *Weka* machine learning library (Hall et al., 2009). Ten-fold cross validation was performed and the outcome was measured using precision, recall and F1-measure.

	Precision	Recall	F1-measure
AnswerPhone	0.836	0.850	0.843
DriveCar	0.803	0.850	0.826
Eat	0.855	0.883	0.869
FightPerson	0.786	0.858	0.821
GetOutCar	0.791	0.725	0.757
HandShake	0.817	0.783	0.800
HugPerson	0.921	0.775	0.842
Kiss	0.783	0.783	0.783
Run	0.939	0.900	0.919
SitDown	0.623	0.675	0.648
SitUp	0.686	0.583	0.631
StandUp	0.483	0.575	0.525
Average	0.777	0.770	0.772

Table 2: Outcomes for the action classification experiment using the Naive Bayes classifier.

5.2 Results

Table 2 presents the outcomes of the monitored classification assessment using *tf-idf* characteristics. The F1 scores for certain categories, such as 'AnswerPhone', 'Eat', 'DriveCar' and 'Run', were greater than some others. For these categories, description concerning humans and the important objects (*e.g.*, dining table, car, phone) were found in most of hand annotations thus classification was not too difficult. In general, F1 scores were higher for categories where human's interaction with an object was evident.

In comparison some categories, such as 'SitDown', 'SitUp' and 'StandUp', had the substantially lower F1 scores than the rest. There were two potential reasons why the annotators did not pay sufficient attention to these actions. Firstly, these actions were performed very quickly in the context of some videos. For example, when a person sat down or stood up during an eating scene, the annotators would have focused on eating (rather than sitting down or standing up) in their description. Secondly, these actions were often overlapped with another action by different humans in the video, which the annotators might have found more important for description. Overall outcome of the classification experiment indicates that the corpus is a reliable tool for assessing natural language description of video streams.

6 Findings from the Corpus Analysis

The corpus is important for the following reasons: (1) limiting this study to a clearly defined and manageable domain; (2) identifying the most important HLFs that should be extracted by image processing techniques in order to describe semantic content of videos; and (3) providing development and test dataset. They should also serve as the ground truths for evaluation.

We have obtained a few insights into the dataset based on the analysis of hand annotations. Annotators are most interested in presence of humans and their attributes in videos, especially their gender, emotions, actions and their interaction with other humans and objects. Based on these observations, we derive a list of HLFs for automatic extraction, consisting of humans and their age, gender, emotion, action, the number of humans, objects, scene setting, spatial and temporal relations. Hand annotation of one visual scene can vary substantially due to the subjectivity of individuals. It can be argued that the dissimilarity lies in the choice of words and that the similarity can be found in the contents that are described. Hand annotations can be used as a reference to evaluate the information content of machine generated descriptions.

7 Conclusion and Future Work

We have developed a new corpus, consisting of natural language descriptions for video data. 12 annotators produced a title and a full description for each of 120 video segments, derived from a subset of Hollywood2 dataset. They are much longer streaming videos than existing ones that were previously annotated with natural language descriptions. As a consequence each segment contains numerous instances of a variety of actions that may overlap in time and occur at various spatial positions within the frame, hence providing a challenge in processing the contents spatially and temporally. The accompanied annotation delineates not only a type of action but also its spatial position and temporal extent. Analysis of this corpus presents insights into human interests and thoughts in such visual scenes. Important visual entities have been identified, aiming at future use for automatic extraction of visual features, which are then used for automatic generation of natural language descriptions for that visual scene.

Acknowledgements. The first author would like to thank Taibah University, Medina, Saudi Arabia for funding this work as part of her PhD scholarship program.

References

James F Allen and George Ferguson. 1994. Actions and events in interval temporal logic. *Journal of logic and computation*, 4(5):531–579.

Moshe Blank, Lena Gorelick, Eli Shechtman, Michal Irani, and Ronen Basri. 2005. Actions as space-time shapes. In *Computer Vision, 2005. ICCV 2005. Tenth IEEE International Conference on*, volume 2, pages 1395–1402. IEEE.

J. Cohen. 1960. A Coefficient of Agreement for Nominal Scales. *Educational and Psychological Measurement*, 20(1):37.

Anthony G Cohn, Jochen Renz, et al. 2008. Qualitative spatial representation and reasoning. *Handbook of knowledge representation*, 3:551–596.

Susan Dumais, John Platt, David Heckerman, and Mehran Sahami. 1998. Inductive learning algorithms and representations for text categorization. In *Proceedings of the seventh international conference on Information and knowledge management*, pages 148–155. ACM.

Paul Ekman. 1992. An argument for basic emotions. *Cognition & emotion*, 6(3-4):169–200.

Barbara J Flood. 1999. Historical note: the start of a stop list at biological abstracts. *Journal of the American Society for Information Science*, 50(12):1066–1066.

Michael Gygli, Helmut Grabner, Hayko Riemenschneider, and Luc Van Gool. 2014. Creating Summaries from User Videos. In *ECCV*.

Mark Hall, Eibe Frank, Geoffrey Holmes, Bernhard Pfahringer, Peter Reutemann, and Ian H Witten. 2009. The weka data mining software: an update. *ACM SIGKDD explorations newsletter*, 11(1):10–18.

Martin F Porter. 1980. An algorithm for suffix stripping. *Program*, 14(3):130–137.

James Pustejovsky, José M Castano, Robert Ingria, Roser Sauri, Robert J Gaizauskas, Andrea Setzer, Graham Katz, and Dragomir R Radev. 2003. Timeml: Robust specification of event and temporal expressions in text. *New directions in question answering*, 3:28–34.

Michaela Regneri, Marcus Rohrbach, Dominikus Wetzel, Stefan Thater, Bernt Schiele, and Manfred Pinkal. 2013. Grounding action descriptions in videos. *Transactions of the Association for Computational Linguistics (TACL)*, 1:25–36.

C. Schuldt, I. Laptev, and B. Caputo. 2004. Recognizing human actions: a local SVM approach. In *Proceedings of ICPR*, volume 3, pages 32–36.

Carl Vondrick, Donald Patterson, and Deva Ramanan. 2013. Efficiently scaling up crowdsourced video annotation. *International Journal of Computer Vision*, 101(1):184–204.

Haonan Yu and Jeffrey Mark Siskind. 2013. Grounded language learning from video described with sentences. In *ACL (1)*, pages 53–63.

Interactively learning visually grounded word meanings from a human tutor

Yanchao Yu
Interaction Lab
Heriot-Watt University
`y.yu@hw.ac.uk`

Arash Eshghi
Interaction Lab
Heriot-Watt University
`a.eshghi@hw.ac.uk`

Oliver Lemon
Interaction Lab
Heriot-Watt University
`o.lemon@hw.ac.uk`

Abstract

We present a multi-modal dialogue system for interactive learning of perceptually grounded word meanings from a human tutor. The system integrates an incremental, semantic parsing/generation framework - Dynamic Syntax and Type Theory with Records (DS-TTR) - with a set of visual classifiers that are learned throughout the interaction and which ground the meaning representations that it produces. We use this system in interaction with a simulated human tutor to study the effect of different dialogue policies and capabilities on accuracy of learned meanings, learning rates, and efforts/costs to the tutor. We show that the overall performance of the learning agent is affected by (1) who takes initiative in the dialogues; (2) the ability to express/use their confidence level about visual attributes; and (3) the ability to process elliptical as well as incrementally constructed dialogue turns.

1 Introduction

Identifying, classifying, and talking about objects or events in the surrounding environment are key capabilities for intelligent, goal-driven systems that interact with other agents and the external world (e.g. robots, smart spaces, and other automated systems). To this end, there has recently been a surge of interest and significant progress made on a variety of related tasks, including generation of Natural Language (NL) descriptions of images, or identifying images based on NL descriptions e.g. (Bruni et al., 2014; Socher et al., 2014). Another strand of work has focused on learning to generate object descriptions and object classification based on low level concepts/features (such as colour, shape and material), enabling systems to identify and describe novel, unseen images

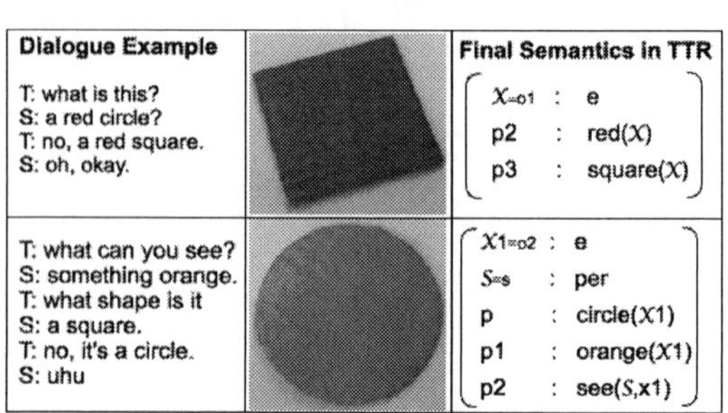

Figure 1: Example dialogues

(Farhadi et al., 2009; Silberer and Lapata, 2014; Sun et al., 2013).

Our goal is to build *interactive* systems that can learn grounded word meanings relating to their perceptions of real-world objects – this is different from previous work such as e.g. (Roy, 2002), that learn groundings from descriptions without any interaction, and more recent work using Deep Learning methods (e.g. (Socher et al., 2014)).

Most of these systems using machine learning rely on training data of high quantity with no possibility of online error correction. Furthermore, they are unsuitable for robots and multimodal systems that need to continuously, and incrementally learn from the environment, and may encounter objects they haven't seen in training data. These limitations should be alleviated if systems can learn concepts as and when needed, from situated dialogue with humans. Interaction with human tutors also enables systems to take initiative and seek information they need by e.g. asking questions with the highest information gain (see e.g. (Skocaj et al., 2011), and Fig. 1). For example, a robot could ask questions (Cakmak and Thomaz, 2012) to learn the colour of a "square" or to request to be presented with more "red" things to improve its performance on the concept (see e.g. Fig. 1). Furthermore, such systems could allow for meaning negotiation in the form of clarifica-

Proceedings of the 5th Workshop on Vision and Language, pages 48–53,
Berlin, Germany, August 12 2016. ©2016 Association for Computational Linguistics

tion interactions with the tutor.

This setting means that the system must be *trainable from little data, compositional, adaptive, and able to handle natural human dialogue with all its glorious context-sensitivity and messiness* – for instance so that it can learn visual concepts suitable for specific tasks/domains, or even those specific to a particular user. Interactive systems that learn continuously, and over the long run from humans need to do so *incrementally*, *quickly*, and *with minimal effort/cost to human tutors*.

In this paper, we use an implemented dialogue system (see Yu et al. (2016b) and architecture in figure 2) that integrates an incremental, semantic grammar framework, especially suited to dialogue processing – Dynamic Syntax and Type Theory with Records (DS-TTR[1] (Kempson et al., 2001; Eshghi et al., 2012)) with visual classifiers which are learned during the interaction, and which provide perceptual grounding for the basic semantic atoms in the semantic representations (Record Types in TTR) produced by the parser (see Fig. 1).

We use this system in interaction with a simulated human tutor, to test hypotheses about how the accuracy of learned meanings, learning rates, and the overall cost/effort for the human tutor are affected by different dialogue policies and capabilities; specifically: (1) who takes initiative in the dialogues; (2) the agent's ability to utilise their level of uncertainty about an object's attributes; and (3) their ability to process elliptical as well as incrementally constructed dialogue turns. The results show that differences along these dimensions have significant impact both on the accuracy of the learned, grounded word meanings, and the processing effort required by the tutors.

2 Related work

Please see (Yu et al., 2016b) for a full discussion of related work. Most similar to our work is probably that of Kennington & Schlangen (2015) who learn a mapping between individual words - rather than logical atoms - and low-level visual features (e.g. colour-values) directly. The system is compositional, yet does not use a grammar (the compositions are defined by hand). Further, the groundings are learned from pairings of object references in NL and images rather than from dialogue.

What sets our approach apart from others is: a) that we use a domain-general, incremental se-

mantic grammar with principled mechanisms for parsing and generation; b) Given DS model of dialogue (Eshghi et al., 2015), representations are constructed jointly and interactively by the tutor and system over the course of several turns (see Fig. 1); c) perception and NL-semantics are modelled in a single logical formalism (TTR); d) we effectively induce an ontology of atomic types in TTR, which can be combined in arbitrarily complex ways for generation of complex descriptions of arbitrarily complex visual scenes (see e.g. (Dobnik et al., 2012) and compare this with (Kennington and Schlangen, 2015), who do not use a grammar and therefore do not have logical structure over grounded meanings).

3 Experimental Setup

Our goal in this paper is an experimental study of the effect of different dialogue policies and capabilities on the overall performance of the learning agent, which, as we describe below is a measure that combines accuracy of learned meanings with the cost of tutoring over time.

Design. We use the dialogue system outlined above to carry out our main experiment with a $2 \times 2 \times 2$ factorial design, i.e. with three factors each with two levels. Together, these factors determine the learner's dialogue behaviour: (1) **Initiative** (**L**earner/**T**utor): determines who takes initiative in the dialogues. When the tutor takes initiative, s/he is the one that drives the conversation forward, by asking questions to the learner (e.g. "What colour is this?" or "So this is a ....") or making a statement about the attributes of the object. On the other hand, when the learner has initiative, it makes statements, asks questions, initiates topics etc. (2) **Uncertainty** (**+UC/-UC**): determines whether the learner takes into account, in its dialogue behaviour, its own subjective confidence about the attributes of the presented object. The confidence is the probability assigned by any of its attribute classifiers of the object being a positive instance of an attribute (e.g. 'red') - see below for how a confidence threshold is used here. In +UC, the agent will not ask a question if it is confident about the answer, and it will hedge the answer to a tutor question if it is not confident, e.g. "T: What is this? L: errm, maybe a square?". In -UC, the agent always takes itself to know the attributes of the given object (as given by its currently trained

---

[1] Download from http://dylan.sourceforge.net

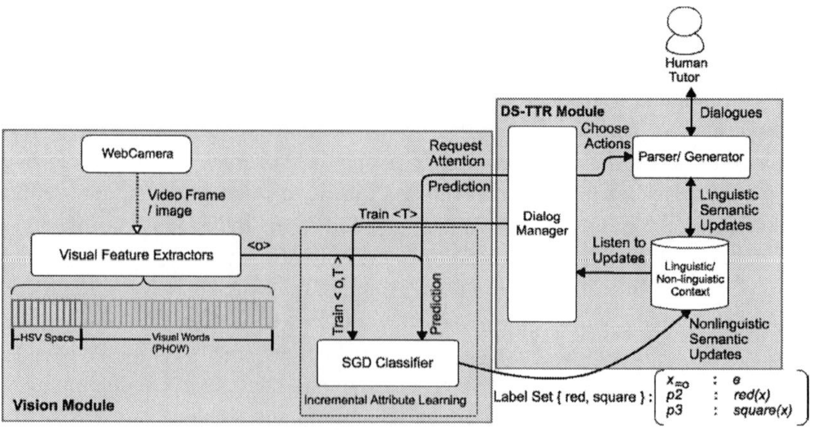

Figure 2: Architecture of the teachable system, see (Yu et al., 2016b)

T+UC+CD	T-UC-CD	T+UC-CD	L+UC+CD
T: This is a ...	T: What (shape) is this?	T: What is this?	L: What colour is this?
L: Errm, a square?	L: This is a circle.	L: Sorry, I don't know.	T: Red.
T: Yes.	T: Yes. What colour is it?	T: Okay, it is a square.	L: Okay.
T: What colour is it?	L: it is red.	L: Okay, I see.	L: is this a square?
L: Red.	T: No, it's purple.	T: What colour is it?	T: No, a circle.
T: No, it's green.	L: Okay, I see.	L: Is it blue?	L: Okay.
L: Okay, thanks.		T: Yes.	

Figure 3: Example dialogues in different conditions

classifiers), and behaves according to that assumption. (3) **Context-Dependency (+CD/-CD)**: determines whether the learner can process (produce/parse) context-dependent expressions such as short answers and incrementally constructed turns, e.g. "T: What is this? L: a square", or "T: So this one is ...? L: red/a circle". This setting can be turned off/on in the DS-TTR dialogue model.

Tutor Simulation and Policy: To run our experiment on a large-scale, we have hand-crafted an *Interactive Tutoring Simulator*, which simulates the behaviour of a human tutor. The tutor policy is kept constant across all conditions. Its policy is that of an always *truthful*, *helpful* and *omniscient* one: it (1) has complete access to the labels of each object; and (2) always acts as the context of the dialogue dictates: answers any question asked, confirms or rejects when the learner describes an object; and (3) always corrects the learner when it describes an object erroneously.

Confidence Threshold: To determine when and how the agent properly copes with its attribute-based predictions, we use confidence-score thresholds. It consists of two values, a base threshold (e.g. 0.5) and a positive threshold (e.g. 0.9).

If the confidences of all classifiers are under the base threshold (i.e. the learner has no attribute label that it is confident about), the agent will ask for information directly from the tutor via questions (e.g. "L: what is this?").

On the other hand, if one or more classifiers score above the base threshold, then the positive threshold is used to judge to what extent the agent trusts its prediction or not. If the confidence score of a classifier is between the positive and base thresholds, the learner is not very confident about its knowledge, and will check with the tutor, e.g. "L: is this red?". However, if the confidence score of a classifier is above the positive threshold, the learner is confident enough in its knowledge not to bother verifying it with the tutor. This will lead to less effort needed from the tutor as the learner becomes more confident about its knowledge.

However, since a learner with high confidence will not ask for assistance from the tutor, a low positive threshold may reduce the chances that allow the tutor to correct the learner's mistakes. Hence, we set up an auxiliary experiment, in which we kept all other conditions constant (i.e. assume that the learner has initiative (**L**) and always considers the prediction confidence(**+U**)), but only varied the threshold values. This additional experiment determined a 0.5 base threshold and a 0.9 positive threshold as the most appropriate values for an interactive learning process - i.e.

Table 1: Recognition Score Table

	Yes	LowYes	LowNo	No
Yes	1	0.5	-0.5	-1
No	-1	-0.5	0.5	1

Table 2: Tutoring Cost Table

C_{inf}	C_{ack}	C_{crt}	$C_{parsing}$	$C_{production}$
1	0.25	1	0.5	1

this preserved good classifier accuracy while not requiring much effort from the tutor.

Recognition score: We follow metrics proposed by Skocaj et al. (2009). 'Recognition score' measures the overall accuracy of the learned word meanings / classifiers, which "rewards successful classifications (i.e. true positives and true negatives) and penalizes incorrect predictions (i.e. false positives and false negatives)" (Skočaj et al., 2009). As the proposed system considers both correctness of predicted labels and prediction confidence on learning tasks, the measure will also take the true labels with lower confidence into account, as shown in Table 1; "LowYes" means that the system made positive predictions but with lower confidence. In this case, the system can generate a polar question to request tutor feedback. "LowNo" is similar to "LowYes", but for negative predictions.

Cost: This measure reflects the effort needed by a human tutor in interacting with the system. Skocaj et. al. (2009) point out that a teachable system should learn as autonomously as possible, rather than involving the human tutor too frequently. There are several possible costs that the tutor might incur, see Table 2: C_{inf} refers to the cost of the tutor providing information on a single attribute (e.g. "this is red" or "this is a square"); C_{ack} is the cost for a simple confirmation (like "yes", "right") or rejection (such as "no"); C_{crt} is the cost of correction for a single concept (e.g. "no, it is blue"). We associate a higher cost with correction of statements than that of polar questions. This is to penalise the learning agent when it confidently makes a false statement – thereby incorporating an aspect of trust in the metric (humans will not trust systems which confidently make false statements). And finally, parsing (C_{parse}) as well as production ($C_{production}$) costs for tutor are taken into account: each single word costs 0.5 when parsed by the tutor, and 1 if generated (production costs twice as much as parsing).

Performance Score: As mentioned above, an efficient learner dialogue policy should consider both classification accuracy (Recognition score)

and tutor effort (Cost). We thus define an integrated measure – the *Overall Performance Ratio* (R_{perf}) – that we use to compare the learner's overall performance across the different conditions:

$$R_{perf} = \frac{\Delta S_{recog}}{C_{tutor}}$$

i.e. the increase in Recognition Score (S_{recog}) per unit of the cost, or equivalently the gradient of the curve in Fig. 4c. We seek dialogue strategies that maximise this.

3.1 Evaluation and Cross-validation

We performed a 20-fold cross validation with 500 images for training and 100 for testing (see (Yu et al., 2016b) for details of the dataset). For each training instance, the learning system interacts (only through dialogue) with the simulated tutor. Each interaction episode ends either when both the shape and the colour of the object are agreed upon, or when the learner requests to be presented with the next image. We define a learning step as comprised of 10 such episodes. At the end of each learning step, the system is tested using the test set. The values used for the Tutoring Cost and the Recognition Score at each learning step correspond to averages across the 20 folds.

4 Results

Fig. 3 shows example interactions between the learner and the tutor in some of the experimental conditions. Note how the system is able to deal with (parse and generate) utterance continuations as in $T+UC+CD$, short answers as in $L+UC+CD$, and polar answers as in $T + UC + CD$.

Fig. 4 plots Recognition Score against Tutoring Cost directly. Note that it is expected that the curves should not terminate in the same place on the x-axis since the different conditions incur different total costs for the tutor. The gradient of this curve corresponds to *increase in Recognition Score per unit of the Tutoring Cost*. It is the gradient of the line drawn from the beginning to the end of each curve ($tan(\beta)$ on Fig. 4) that constitutes our main evaluation measure of the system's overall performance in each condition, and it is this measure for which we report statistical significance re-

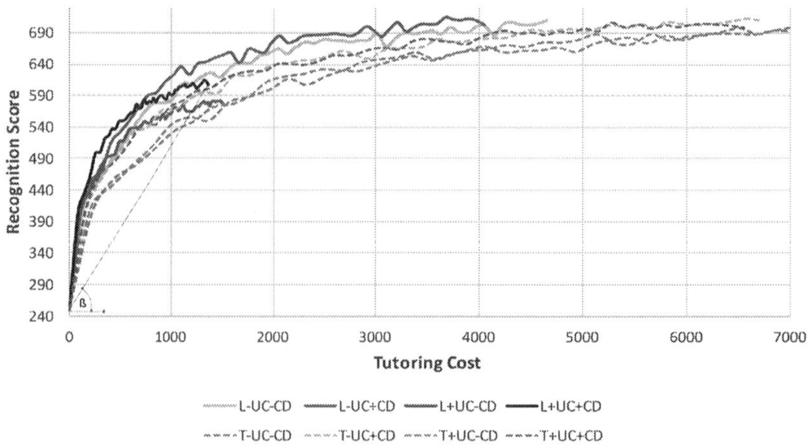

Figure 4: Evolution of Overall Learning Performance

sults: a between-subjects ANOVA shows significant main effects of Initiative ($p < 0.01; F = 469.2$), Uncertainty ($p < 0.01; F = 179.8$) and Context-Dependency ($p < 0.01; F = 20.12$) on the system's overall performance. There is also a significant Initiative×Uncertainty interaction ($p < 0.01; F = 181.72$).

5 Discussion

The cumulative cost for the tutor progresses more slowly when the learner has initiative (L) and takes its confidence into account in its behaviour (+UC). This is so because *a form of active learning* is taking place here: the learner only asks a question about attribute if it isn't confident enough already about that attribute. As the agent is exposed to more training instances its subjective confidence about its own predictions increases over time, and thus there is progressively less need for tutoring. On the other hand, the Recognition Score increases more slowly too in the L+UC conditions. This is because the agent's confidence score in the beginning is unreliable as it has only seen a few training instances: in many cases it doesn't have any interaction with the tutor and so there are informative examples that it doesn't get exposed to.

However, comparing the gradients of the two curves on Fig. 4 shows that the above trade-off between Recognition Score and Cost is in fact a good one: the overall performance of the agent is significantly better in the L+UC conditions (recall the Initiative × Uncertainty interaction). The significant main effect of Context-Dependency on overall performance is explained by the fact that in +CD conditions, the agent can process context-dependent and incrementally constructed turns, leading to less repetition, shorter dialogues, and so better overall performance.

6 Conclusion and Future work

We have presented a multi-modal dialogue system that learns grounded word meanings from a human tutor, incrementally, over time. The system integrates a semantic grammar for dialogue (DS), a logical theory of types (TTR), with a set of visual classifiers in which the TTR semantic representations are grounded. We used this implemented system to study the effect of different dialogue policies and capabilities on the overall performance of a learning agent - a combined measure of accuracy and cost. The results show that in order to maximise its performance, the agent needs to take initiative in the dialogues, take into account its confidence about its predictions, and be able to process natural, human-like dialogue. Ongoing work uses Reinforcement Learning to acquire adaptive dialogue policies that optimise such an agent's performance (Yu et al., 2016a).

Acknowledgements

This research is supported by the EPSRC, under grant number EP/M01553X/1 (BABBLE project), and by the European Union's Horizon 2020 research and innovation programme under grant agreement No. 688147 (MuMMER [2]).

---

[2]http://mummer-project.eu/

References

Elia Bruni, Nam-Khanh Tran, and Marco Baroni. 2014. Multimodal distributional semantics. *J. Artif. Intell. Res.(JAIR)*, 49(1–47).

Maya Cakmak and Andrea Thomaz. 2012. Designing robot learners that ask good questions. In *Proc. HRI*.

Simon Dobnik, Robin Cooper, and Staffan Larsson. 2012. Modelling language, action, and perception in type theory with records. In *Proceedings of the 7th International Workshop on Constraint Solving and Language Processing (CSLPÄô12)*, pages 51–63.

Arash Eshghi, Julian Hough, Matthew Purver, Ruth Kempson, and Eleni Gregoromichelaki. 2012. Conversational interactions: Capturing dialogue dynamics. In S. Larsson and L. Borin, editors, *From Quantification to Conversation: Festschrift for Robin Cooper on the occasion of his 65th birthday*, volume 19 of *Tributes*, pages 325–349. College Publications, London.

A. Eshghi, C. Howes, E. Gregoromichelaki, J. Hough, and M. Purver. 2015. Feedback in conversation as incremental semantic update. In *Proceedings of the 11th International Conference on Computational Semantics (IWCS 2015)*, London, UK. Association for Computational Linguisitics.

Ali Farhadi, Ian Endres, Derek Hoiem, and David Forsyth. 2009. Describing objects by their attributes. In *Proceedings of the IEEE Computer Society Conference on Computer Vision and Pattern Recognition (CVPR.*

Ruth Kempson, Wilfried Meyer-Viol, and Dov Gabbay. 2001. *Dynamic Syntax: The Flow of Language Understanding*. Blackwell.

Casey Kennington and David Schlangen. 2015. Simple learning and compositional application of perceptually grounded word meanings for incremental reference resolution. In *Proceedings of the Conference for the Association for Computational Linguistics (ACL-IJCNLP)*. Association for Computational Linguistics.

Deb Roy. 2002. A trainable visually-grounded spoken language generation system. In *Proceedings of the International Conference of Spoken Language Processing*.

Carina Silberer and Mirella Lapata. 2014. Learning grounded meaning representations with autoencoders. In *Proceedings of the 52nd Annual Meeting of the Association for Computational Linguistics (Volume 1: Long Papers)*, volume 1, pages 721–732, Baltimore, Maryland, June. Association for Computational Linguistics.

Danijel Skocaj, Matej Kristan, Alen Vrecko, Marko Mahnic, Miroslav Janícek, Geert-Jan M. Kruijff, Marc Hanheide, Nick Hawes, Thomas Keller, Michael Zillich, and Kai Zhou. 2011. A system for interactive learning in dialogue with a tutor. In *2011 IEEE/RSJ International Conference on Intelligent Robots and Systems, IROS 2011, San Francisco, CA, USA, September 25-30, 2011*, pages 3387–3394.

Danijel Skočaj, Matej Kristan, and Aleš Leonardis. 2009. Formalization of different learning strategies in a continuous learning framework. In *Proceedings of the Ninth International Conference on Epigenetic Robotics; Modeling Cognitive Development in Robotic Systems*, pages 153–160. Lund University Cognitive Studies.

Richard Socher, Andrej Karpathy, Quoc V Le, Christopher D Manning, and Andrew Y Ng. 2014. Grounded compositional semantics for finding and describing images with sentences. *Transactions of the Association for Computational Linguistics*, 2:207–218.

Yuyin Sun, Liefeng Bo, and Dieter Fox. 2013. Attribute based object identification. In *Robotics and Automation (ICRA), 2013 IEEE International Conference on*, pages 2096–2103. IEEE.

Yanchao Yu, Arash Eshghi, and Oliver Lemon. 2016a. Training an adaptive dialogue policy for interactive learning of visually grounded word meanings. In *(under review)*.

Yanchao Yu, Oliver Lemon, and Arash Eshghi. 2016b. Comparing dialogue strategies for learning grounded language from human tutor. In *Proc. SEMDIAL 2016*.

Pragmatic factors in image description: the case of negations

Emiel van Miltenburg
Vrije Universiteit Amsterdam
`emiel.van.miltenburg@vu.nl`

Roser Morante
Vrije Universiteit Amsterdam
`roser.morante@vu.nl`

Desmond Elliott
ILLC, University of Amsterdam
`d.elliott@uva.nl`

Abstract

We provide a qualitative analysis of the descriptions containing negations (*no, not, n't, nobody*, etc) in the Flickr30K corpus, and a categorization of negation uses. Based on this analysis, we provide a set of requirements that an image description system should have in order to generate negation sentences. As a pilot experiment, we used our categorization to manually annotate sentences containing negations in the Flickr30k corpus, with an agreement score of κ=0.67. With this paper, we hope to open up a broader discussion of subjective language in image descriptions.

1 Introduction

Descriptions of images are typically collected from untrained workers via crowdsourcing platforms, such as Mechanical Turk[1]. The workers are explicitly instructed to describe only what they can see in the image, in an attempt to control content selection (Young et al., 2014; Chen et al., 2015). However, workers are still free to project their world view when writing the descriptions and they make linguistic choices, such as using negation structures (van Miltenburg, 2016).

In this paper we study the use of *negations* in image descriptions. A negation is a word that communicates that something is *not* the case. Negations are often used when there is a mismatch between what speakers expect to be the case and what is actually the case (see e.g. (Leech, 1983; Beukeboom et al., 2010)). For example, if Queen Elizabeth of England were to appear in public wearing jeans instead of a dress, (1a) would be acceptable because she is known to wear dresses

in public. But if she were to show up wearing a dress, (1b) would be unexpected.

(1) a.　Queen Elizabeth isn't wearing a dress
　　 b. ??Queen Elizabeth isn't wearing jeans

Thus the correct use of negations often requires *background knowledge*, or at least some sense of what is expected and what is not.

We focus on two kinds of negations: **non-affixal negations** (*not, n't, never, no, none, nothing, nobody, nowhere, nor, neither*) (Tottie, 1980); and **implicit negations** in the form of prepositions (*without, sans,* and *minus*), and the verbs *lack, omit, miss* and *fail.* Horn (1989) calls this second category 'inherent negatives'. Affixal negations (words starting with *a–, dis–, un–, non–, un–* or ending with *–less*) are beyond the scope of this paper, but we hope to address them in future work.

The main contributions of this paper are an overview of different uses of negations in image description corpora, analysing the background knowledge required to generate negations, and the implications for image description models.[2]

2 Data

We focus on negations on the Flickr30K dataset (Young et al., 2014). The negations were detected by lexical string-matching using regular expressions, except for the verbs. For the verbs, we checked if any of the tokens starts with *lack, omit, miss* or *fail.* Our search yielded 896 sentences, of which 892 unique, and 31 false positives. Table 1 shows frequency counts for each negation term.

We carried out the same analysis for the Microsoft COCO dataset (Chen et al., 2015) to see if the proportion of negations is a constant. Our approach yielded 3339 sentences on the training and

---

[1]`http://www.mturk.com`

[2]We provide all of our code, data, and annotation guidelines online. See: `https://github.com/evanmilte` `nburg/annotating-negations`

Proceedings of the 5th Workshop on Vision and Language, pages 54–59,
Berlin, Germany, August 12 2016. ©2016 Association for Computational Linguistics

no	371	nothing	16	neither	2
not	198	lack	9	sans	1
without	141	fail	9	none	1
miss	69	never	5	nobody	1
n't	68	nowhere	3		

Table 1: Frequency counts for each negation term.

validation splits, of which 3232 unique. The presence of negations appears to be a linear function of dataset size: 0.56% in the Flickr30K dataset, and 0.54% in the MS COCO dataset. This suggests that the use of negations is not particular to either dataset, but rather it is a robust phenomenon across datasets.

Table 2 shows the distribution of descriptions containing negations across images. In the majority of cases only one of the five descriptions contains a negation (86.25% in Flickr30K and 72.05% in MS COCO). Only in very exceptional cases do the five descriptions contain negations. This indicates that the use of negation is a subjective choice.

Dataset	1	2	3	4	5
Flickr30K	659	85	16	1	3
MS COCO	2406	277	78	30	5

Table 2: Distribution of the number of descriptions of an image with at least one negation term.

3 Negation uses in image descriptions

In this section, we provide a categorization of negation uses and assess the amount of required background knowledge for each use. Our categorization is the result of manually inspecting all the data twice: the first time to develop a taxonomy, and the second time to apply this taxonomy to all 892 sentences. Note that our categorization is meant as a *practical guide* to be of use for natural language generation. There is already a unifying explanation for *why* people use negations (unexpectedness, see (Leech, 1983; Beukeboom et al., 2010)). The question here is *how* people use negations, what they negate, and what kind of knowledge is required to produce those negations.

Salient absence: The first use of negation is to indicate that something is absent:

(2) a. A man **without** a shirt playing tennis.

    b. A woman at graduation **without** a cap on.

Shirts and shoes are most commonly mentioned as being absent in the Flickr30K dataset. From examples like (2a) speaks the norm that people are supposed to be fully dressed. These examples seem common enough for a machine to learn the association between exposed chests and the phrase *without a shirt*. But there are also more difficult cases, such as (2b). To describe an image like this, one should know that students (in the USA) typically wear caps at their graduation. This example shows the importance of background knowledge for the full description of an image.

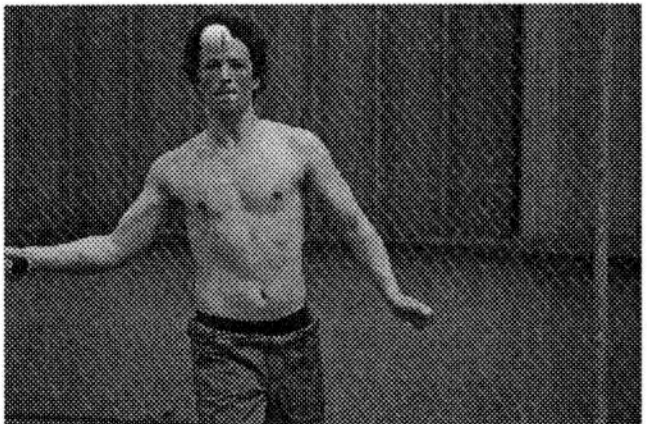

Example 2a (Image 2883099128)

Negation of action/behavior: The second category is the use of negation to deny that an action or some kind of behavior is occurring:

(3) a. A kid eating out of a plate **without** using his hands.

    b. A woman in the picture has fallen down and **no** one is stopping to help her up.

Examples like these require an understanding of what is likely or supposed to happen, or how people are expected to behave.

Example 3a (Image 39397486)

Negation of property: The next use of negation is to note that an entity in the image lacks a property. In (4a), the negation does two things: it highlights that the buildings are not finished, but in its combination with *yet* suggests that they *will be* finished.

55

(4) a. A man wearing a hard hat stands in front of buildings **not** yet finished being built.

   b. There are four boys playing soccer, but **not** all of them are on the same team [...].

In (4b), the negated phrase also performs two roles: it communicates that there are (at least) two teams, and it denies that the four boys are all in the same team. For both examples, the negated parts (*being finished* and *being on the same team*) are properties associated with the concepts of BUILD-ING and PLAYING TOGETHER, and could reasonably be expected to be true of buildings and groups of boys playing soccer. The negations ensure that these expectations are cancelled.

Example 4a (Image 261883591)

Example (5) shows a completely different effect of negating a property. Here, the negation is used to *compare* the depicted situation with a particular *reference point*. The implication here is that the picture is not taken in the USA.

(5) A wild animal **not** found in america jumping through a field.

Negation of attitude: The fourth use of nega-tion concerns attitudes of entities toward actions or others. The examples in (6) illustrate that this use requires an understanding of emotions or at-titudes, but also some reasoning about what those emotions are directed at.

(6) a. A man sitting on a panel **not** enjoying the speech.

   b. The dog in the picture does**n't** like blowing dryer.

Example 6a (Image 2313609814)

Outside the frame: The most image-specific use of negation is to note that particular entities are not depicted or out of focus:

(7) a. A woman is taking a picture of something **not** in the shot with her phone.

   b. Several people sitting in front of a building taking pictures of a landmark **not** seen.

The use of negation in this category requires an understanding of the events taking place in the image, and what entities might be involved in such events. (7b) is a particularly interesting case, where the annotator specifically says that there is a *landmark* outside the frame. This raises the ques-tion: how does she know and how could a com-puter algorithm recognise this?

Example 7a (Image 4895028664)

(Preventing) future events: The sixth use of negation concerns future events, generally with people preventing something from happening. Here are two examples:

(8) a. A man is riding a bucking horse trying to hold on and **not** get thrown off.

   b. A girl tries holding onto a vine so she wo**n't** fall into the water.

What is interesting about these sentences is that the ability to produce them does not only require an understanding of the depicted situation (some-one is holding on to a horse/vine), but also of the possibilities within that situation (they may or may not fall off/into the water), depending on the ac-tions taken.

Example 8a (Image 263428541)

Quotes and Idioms: Some instances of negations are *mentions* rather than *uses* as shown in (9).

(9) A girl with a tattoo on her wrist that reads "**no regrets**" has her hand outstretched.

Other times, the use of a negation isn't concerned with the image as much as it is with the English language. The examples in (10) illustrate this *idiomatic* or *conventional* use of negation.

(10) a. Strolling down path to **nowhere**.
    b. Three young boys are engaged in a game of do**n't** drop the melon.

Example 10a (Image 4870785283)

Other: Several sentences do not fit in any of the above categories, but there aren't enough similar examples to merit a category of their own. Two examples are given below. In (11), the negation is used to convey that it is *atypical* to be holding an umbrella when it is not raining.

(11) The little boy [...] is smiling under the blue umbrella even though it is **not** raining.

Example 11 (Image 371522748)

In (12), the annotator recognized the intention of the toddler, and is using the negation to contrast the goals with the ability of the toddler. Though there are many other sentences where the negation is used to contrast two parts of the sentence (see Section 4), there is just one example where an *ability* is negated.

(12) A little toddler trying to look through a scope but ca**n't** reach it.

We expect have no doubt that there are still other kinds of examples in the Flickr30K and the MS COCO datasets. Future research should assess the degree to which the current taxonomy is sufficient to systematically study the production of negations in image descriptions.

4   Annotating the Flickr30K corpus

Two of the authors annotated the Flickr30K corpus using the categories listed above with two goals: to validate the categories, and to develop annotation guidelines for future work. By going through all sentences with negations, we were able to identify borderline cases that could serve as examples in the final guidelines.

Using the categories defined in Section 3, we achieved an inter-annotator agreement of Cohen's κ=0.67, with an agreement of 77%. We then looked at sentences with disagreement, and settled on categories for those sentences. Table 3 shows the final counts for each category, including a Meta-category for cases like *I don't see a picture*, commenting on the original annotation task, or on the images without describing them.

Category	Count
Salient absence	488
Negation of action/behavior	90
Quotes and idioms	71
Not a description/Meta	40
Negation of attitude	36
False positive	31
Outside the frame	26
Negation of property	25
(Preventing) future events	21
Other	66

Table 3: Frequency count of each category.

In addition to our categorization, we found 39 examples where negations are also used to provide **contrast** (next to their use in terms of the categories listed above). Two examples are:

(13) a. A man shaves his neck but **not** his beard
    b. A man in a penguin suit runs with a man, **not** in a penguin suit

Such examples show how negations can be used to structure an image. Sometimes this leads to a scalar implicature (Horn, 1972), like in (14).

(14) Three teenagers, two **without** shoes having
a water gun fight with various types of guns
trying to spray each other.

⇒ One teenager *is* wearing shoes.

A striking observation is that many negations
pertain to pieces of clothing; for example: 282
(32%) of the negations are about people being
shirtless, while 59 (7%) are about people not wearing shoes. It is unclear whether this is due to selection bias, or whether the world just contains many
shirtless people. But we expect that this distribution will make it difficult for systems to learn how
to use negations that aren't clothing-related.

5 Discussion

The negations used by crowdworkers are likely to
have required some form of "world knowledge".
We now discuss potential sources of evidence for
recognising a candidate for negation in the description of an image: (a) The *Outside the frame*
category requires an understanding of human gaze
within an image, which is a challenging problem
in computer vision (Valenti et al., 2012). Additionally, we also need to understand the differences between scene types, both from a compu-
tational- (Oliva and Torralba, 2001) and a human
perspective (Torralba et al., 2006). (b) The *Salient
absence* category provides evidence for two kinds
of expectations that play a role in the use of negations: general expectations (people are supposed
to wear shirts, cf. 2a) and situation-specific expectations (students at graduation ceremonies typically wear caps, cf. 2b). (c) Finally, the *Negation
of action/behavior* category requires action recognition, which is a challenging problem in still images (Poppe, 2010). The ability to automatically
recognise what people are doing in an image, and
how this contrasts with what they would typically
do in similar images, would greatly help with generating this use of negation.

From a linguistic perspective, background
knowledge could be represented by *frames* (Fillmore, 1976) and *scripts* (Schank and Abelson,
1977). There are some hand-crafted resources that
contain this kind of knowledge, e.g. FrameNet
(Baker et al., 1998), but they only have limited
coverage. Recent work has shown, however, that it
is possible to automatically learn frames (Pennacchiotti et al., 2008) and script knowledge (Chambers and Jurafsky, 2009) from text corpora. Fast
et al. (2016) show how such knowledge, as well

as knowledge about *object affordances* (Gibson,
1977), can be used to reason about visual scenes.

6 Conclusion

We studied the use of negations in the Flickr30K
dataset. The use of negations imply that the descriptions contain a combination of objective and
subjective interpretations of the images. But negations are only one type of subjective language in
image description datasets. We expect that different subjective language use (e.g. discourse mark-
ers such as *yet* or *even though*) can be observed
with relative ease in this and other datasets. Additionally it would be interesting to study the use
of negations in different languages, such as the
German-English Multi30K dataset (Elliott et al.,
2016). We encourage further research to discover
other types of subjective language in vision and
language datasets, and studies of how subjective
language may affect language generation.

7 Acknowledgments

EM and RM are supported by the Netherlands Organization for Scientific Research (NWO) via the
Spinoza-prize awarded to Piek Vossen (SPI 30-
673, 2014-2019). DE is supported by NWO Vici
grant nr. 277-89-002 awarded to Khalil Sima'an.

References

Collin F. Baker, Charles J. Fillmore, and John B. Lowe.
1998. The berkeley framenet project. In *Proceedings of the 36th Annual Meeting of the Association for Computational Linguistics and 17th International Conference on Computational Linguistics -
Volume 1*, ACL '98, pages 86–90, Stroudsburg, PA,
USA. Association for Computational Linguistics.

Camiel J Beukeboom, Catrin Finkenauer, and
Daniël HJ Wigboldus. 2010. The negation bias:
when negations signal stereotypic expectancies.
Journal of personality and social psychology,
99(6):978.

Nathanael Chambers and Dan Jurafsky. 2009. Un-
supervised learning of narrative schemas and their
participants. In *Proceedings of the Joint Conference of the 47th Annual Meeting of the ACL and the
4th International Joint Conference on Natural Language Processing of the AFNLP: Volume 2 - Volume
2*, ACL '09, pages 602–610, Stroudsburg, PA, USA.
Association for Computational Linguistics.

Xinlei Chen, Hao Fang, Tsung-Yi Lin, Ramakrishna Vedantam, Saurabh Gupta, Piotr Dollár, and

C. Lawrence Zitnick. 2015. Microsoft COCO captions: Data collection and evaluation server. *CoRR*, abs/1504.00325.

Desmond Elliott, Stella Frank, Khalil Sima'an, and Lucia Specia. 2016. Multi30K: Multilingual English-German Image Descriptions. *CoRR*, abs/1605.00459.

Ethan Fast, William McGrath, Pranav Rajpurkar, and Michael S. Bernstein. 2016. Augur: Mining human behaviors from fiction to power interactive systems. In *Proceedings of the 2016 CHI Conference on Human Factors in Computing Systems*, CHI '16, pages 237–247, New York, NY, USA. ACM.

Charles J Fillmore. 1976. Frame semantics and the nature of language. *Annals of the New York Academy of Sciences*, 280(1):20–32.

James J. Gibson. 1977. The theory of affordances. In R. E. Shaw and J. Bransford, editors, *Perceiving, Acting, and Knowing*. Hillsdale, NJ: Lawrence Erlbaum Associates.

Laurence R. Horn. 1972. *On the Semantic Properties of Logical Operators in English*. Ph.D. thesis, UCLA, Los Angeles.

Laurence R. Horn. 1989. *A natural history of negation*. CSLI Publications.

Geoffrey Leech. 1983. *Principles of pragmatics*. London and New York: Longman.

Aude Oliva and Antonio Torralba. 2001. Modeling the shape of the scene: A holistic representation of the spatial envelope. *International Journal of Computer Vision*, 42(3):145–175.

Marco Pennacchiotti, Diego De Cao, Roberto Basili, Danilo Croce, and Michael Roth. 2008. Automatic induction of framenet lexical units. In *Proceedings of the Conference on Empirical Methods in Natural Language Processing*, pages 457–465. Association for Computational Linguistics.

Ronald Poppe. 2010. A survey on vision-based human action recognition. *Image and Vision Computing*, 28(6):976 – 990.

Roger C. Schank and Robert P. Abelson. 1977. *Scripts, Plans, Goals, and Understanding: An Inquiry Into Human Knowledge Structures*. L. Erlbaum Associates.

Antonio Torralba, Aude Oliva, Monica S Castelhano, and John M Henderson. 2006. Contextual guidance of eye movements and attention in real-world scenes: the role of global features in object search. *Psychological review*, 113(4):766.

Gunnel Tottie. 1980. Affixal and non-affixal negation in English: Two systems in (almost) complementary distribution. *Studia linguistica*, 34(2):101–123.

Roberto Valenti, Nicu Sebe, and Theo Gevers. 2012. Combining head pose and eye location information for gaze estimation. *IEEE Transactions on Image Processing*, 21(2):802–815, Feb.

Emiel van Miltenburg. 2016. Stereotyping and bias in the Flickr30K dataset. In *Proceedings of the 11th Workshop on Multimodal Corpora (MMC2016)*, pages 1–4.

Peter Young, Alice Lai, Micah Hodosh, and Julia Hockenmaier. 2014. From image descriptions to visual denotations: New similarity metrics for semantic inference over event descriptions. *TACL*, 2:67–78.

Building a *bagpipe* with a *bag* and a *pipe*:
Exploring Conceptual Combination in Vision *

Sandro Pezzelle and **Ravi Shekhar**[†] and **Raffaella Bernardi**
CIMeC - Center for Mind/Brain Sciences, University of Trento
[†]DISI, University of Trento
{firstname.lastname}@unitn.it

Abstract

This preliminary study investigates whether, and to what extent, conceptual combination is conveyed by vision. Working with noun-noun compounds we show that, for some cases, the composed visual vector built with a simple additive model is effective in approximating the visual vector representing the complex concept.

1 Introduction

Conceptual combination is the cognitive process by which two or more existing concepts are combined to form new complex concepts (Wisniewski, 1996; Gagné and Shoben, 1997; Costello and Keane, 2000). From a linguistic perspective, this mechanism can be observed in the formation and lexicalization of compound words (eg. *boathouse*, *swordfish*, *headmaster*, etc.), a widespread and very productive linguistic device (Downing, 1977) that is usually defined in literature as the result of the composition of two (or more) existing and free-standing words (Lieber and Štekauer, 2009). Within both perspectives, scholars agree that the composition of concepts/words is something more than a simple addition (Gagné and Spalding, 2006; Libben, 2014). However, additive models turned out to be effective in language, where they have been successfully applied to distributional semantic vectors (Paperno and Baroni, to appear).

Based on these previous findings, the present work addresses the issue of whether, and to what extent, conceptual combination can be described

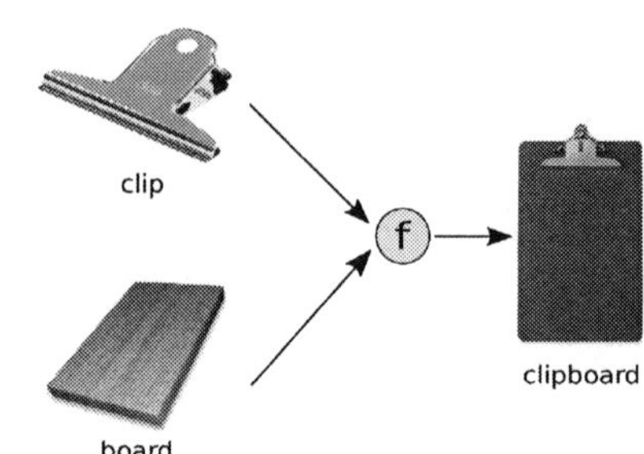

Figure 1: Can we obtain a *clipboard* by combining *clip* and *board* with a compositional function *f*?

in vision as the result of adding together two single concepts. That is, can the visual representation of *clipboard* be obtained by using the visual representations of a *clip* and a *board* as shown in Figure 1? In order to investigate this issue, we experiment with visual features that are extracted from images representing concrete and imageable concepts. More precisely, we use noun-noun compounds for which ratings of imageability are available. The rationale for choosing NN-compounds is that composition should take advantage from dealing with concepts for which clear, well-defined visual representations are available, as it is the case of nouns (representing objects). In particular, we test whether a simple additive model can be applied to vision in a similar fashion to how it has been done for language (Mitchell and Lapata, 2010). We show that for some NN-compounds the visual representation of the whole can be obtained by simply summing up its parts. We also discuss cases where the model fails and provide conjectures for more suitable approaches. Since, to our knowledge, no datasets of images labeled with NN-compounds are currently available, we manually build and make available a preliminary dataset.

*We are grateful to Marco Baroni and Aurélie Herbelot for the valuable advice and feedback. This project has received funding from ERC 2011 Starting Independent Research Grant n. 283554 (COMPOSES). We gratefully acknowledge the support of NVIDIA Corporation with the donation of the GPUs used in our research.

Proceedings of the 5th Workshop on Vision and Language, pages 60–64,
Berlin, Germany, August 12 2016. ©2016 Association for Computational Linguistics

2   Related Works

Recently, there has been a growing interest in combining information from language and vision. The reason lies on the fact that many concepts can be similar in one modality but very different in the other, and thus capitalizing on both information turns out to be very effective in many tasks. Evidence supporting this intuition has been provided by several works (Lazaridou et al., 2015; Johnson et al., 2015; Xiong et al., 2016; Ordonez et al., 2016) that developed multimodal models for representing concepts that outperformed both language-based and vision-based models in different tasks. Multimodal representations have been also used for exploring compositionality in visual objects (Vendrov et al., 2015), but compositionality was intended as combining two or more objects in a visual scene (eg., an apple and a banana) and not as obtaining the representation of a new concept based on two or more existing concepts.

Even though some research in visual compositionality has been carried out for part segmentation tasks (Wang and Yuille, 2015), we focus on a rather unexplored avenue. To our knowledge, the closest work to ours is represented by Nguyen et al. (2014), who used a compositional model of distributional semantics for generating adjective-noun phrases (eg., a *red car* given the vectors of *red* and *car*) both in language and vision. According to their results, a substantial correlation can be found between observed and composed representations in the visual modality. Moving from these results, the present study addresses the issue of whether, and to which extent, a compositional model can be applied to vision for obtaining noun-noun combinations, without relying on linguistic information.

3   Dataset

To test our hypothesis, we used the publicly available dataset by Juhasz et al. (2014). It contains 629 English compounds for which human ratings on overall imageability (ie., a variable measuring the extent to which a compound word evokes a nonverbal image besides a verbal representation) are available. We relied on this measure for carrying out a first filtering of the data, based on the assumption that the more imageable a compound, the clearer and better-defined its visual representation. As a first step, we selected the most imageable items in the list by retaining only the ones

with an average score of at least 5 points in a scale ranging from 1 (e.g., *whatnot*: 1.04) to 7 (e.g., *watermelon*: 6.95). From this subset, including 240 items, one of the authors further selected only genuine noun-noun combinations, so that items like *outfit* or *handout* were discarded. We then queried each compound and its constituent nouns in Google images and we selected only those items for which every object in the tuple (eg. *airplane*, *air*, and *plane*) had a relatively good visual representation by looking at the top 25 images. This step, in particular, was aimed at discarding the surprisingly numerous cases for which only noisy images (ie., representing brands, products, or containing signs) were available.

From the resulting dataset, containing 115 items, we manually selected those that we considered as compositional in vision. As a criterion, only NN-combinations that can be seen as resulting from either combining an object with a background (e.g., *airplane*: a *plane* is somehow superimposed in the *air* background) or concatenating two objects (e.g., *clipboard*) were selected. Such a criterion is consistent with our purpose, that is finding those cases where visual composition works. The rationale is that there should be composition when both the constituent concepts are present in the visual representation of the composed one. Two authors separately carried out the selection procedure, and the few cases for which there was disagreement were resolved by discussion. In total, 38 items were selected and included in what we will heceforth refer to as **compositional group**. Interestingly, the two visual criteria followed by the annotators turned out to partly reflect the kind of semantic relation implicitly tying the two nouns. In particular, most of the selected items hold either a noun2 HAS noun1 (eg., *clipboard*) or a noun2 LOCATED noun1 (eg., *cupcake*) relation according to Levi (1978).

In addition, 12 other compounds (eg., *sunflower*, *footstool*, *rattlesnake*, etc.) were randomly selected from the 115-item subset. We will heceforth refer to this set as the **control group**, whereas we will refer to the concatenation of the two sets (38+12=50 items) as the **full group**. For each compound in the full group, we manually searched images representing it and each of its constituents nouns in Google images. One good image, possibly showing the most prototypical representation of that concept according to the authors' experience, was selected. In total, 79 images for N-constituents plus 50 images for NN-compounds (129 in total) images were included in our dataset.[1]

4 Model

In order to have a clear and interpretable picture of what we obtain when composing visual features of nouns, in this preliminary study we experimented with a simple additive compositional model. Simple additive models can be seen as weighting models applying the same weight to both elements involved. That is, when composing *waste* and *basket*, both nouns are considered as playing the same (visual) role with respect to the overall representation, ie. *wastebasket*. Intuitively enough, we expect this function being effective in approximating visual representations of complex concepts where the parts are still visible (eg., *clipboard*). In contrast, we don't expect good results when the composition requires more abstract, subtle interactions between the nouns (eg., *cannonball*).

To directly compare vision against language, we applied the same compositional function to the linguistic vectors (extracted from large corpora of texts) representing the same dataset. What we expected from such a comparison is a different and possibly complementary behavior: since linguistic vectors encode contexts in which the target word is very likely to occur, language could be more effective in modulating abstract interactions (ie., *cannonball*), whereas vision might be possibly better in composing grounded concepts (ie., *clipboard*). As a consequence, we expect language performing better in the control group, but differently from vision in the compositional group.

4.1 Visual Features

Each image in the dataset is represented by visual features extracted by using state-of-the-art technique based on Convolutional Neural Networks (Simonyan and Zisserman, 2014). We used the VGG-19 model pretrained on the ImageNet ILSVRC data (Russakovsky et al., 2015). The model includes multiple convolutional layers followed by max pooling and the top of these are fully connected layers ($fc6$, $fc7$, $fc8$). We used 4096-dimensional visual vectors extracted from the $fc6$ layer, which has shown better performance

in image retrieval/matching task (Babenko et al., 2014) compared to other layers. For experimental purpose, we used MatConvNet (Vedaldi and Lenc, 2015) toolbox for features extraction.

4.2 Linguistic Features

Each word in the dataset is represented by a 400-dimension vector extracted from a semantic space[2] built with the CBOW architecture implemented in the word2vec toolkit (Mikolov et al., 2013) and the best-performing parameters in Baroni et al. (2014).

5 Evaluation Measures

To evaluate the compositionality of each NN-compound, we measure the extent to which the composed vector is similar to the corresponding observed one, ie. the vector directly extracted from either texts or the selected image. Hence, first of all we use the standard $Cosine$ similarity measure. The higher the similarity, the better the composition. It could be the case that the composed vector is however less similar to the observed one than it is the closest N-constituent. Thus, similarity by its own is not informative of whether the composition function has provided additional information compared to that conveyed by the closest single noun. In order to take into account this issue, we also compute the similarity between the composed vector and both its N-constituents ($N1, N2$). We lower the similarity between the composed and the observed vector by subtracting the similarity between the observed vector and the noun that is closest to it (we call this measure $CompInfo$, since it is informative of the effectiveness of the composition). When the composition operation maps the composed vector closer to the observed vector compared to its constituents in the semantic space, the composition provides more information. In particular, when $CompInfo$ is positive (ie., greater than 0), the composition is considered to be effective.

To further evaluate the compositionality of the nominal compound, we test the effectiveness of the composed vector in the retrieval task. The reason is to double-check the distictiveness of the composed vector with respect to all the objects (ie., 79 N-constituents plus 50 NN-compounds) in

---

[1] The dataset is publicly available and can be downloaded at https://github.com/shekharRavi/

[2] The corpus used for building the semantic space is a 2.8 billion tokens concatenation of the web-derived ukWac, a mid-2009 dump of the English Wikipedia, and the British National Corpus.

Table 1: Compositionality evaluation in Vision and Language.

Dataset	$Avg.Similarity$		$\%(CompInfo > 0)$		$Rec@1$		$Rec@5$	
	Vision	Lang	Vision	Lang	Vision	Lang	Vision	Lang
Full	0.6283	0.407	62%	72%	0.34	0.52	0.76	0.88
Compositional	0.6476	0.429	76.31%	76.31%	0.3947	0.57889	0.8158	0.9211
Control	0.5671	0.3377	16.66%	58.33%	0.1667	0.3333	0.5833	0.75

the semantic space. Using the composed vector as query, we are interested in knowing the rank of the corresponding observed vector. Since for each query there is only one correct item in the whole semantic space, the most informative retrieval measure is Recall. Hence, we evaluate compositionality by $Rec@k$. Since we have already scrutinized the role of the N-constituents with the previous measure, in the retrieval of a NN-compound both its N-constituents are removed from the semantic space. The same evaluation is conducted for both vision and language, thus providing a way to directly compare the two modalities.

6 Results

In Table 1, we report average similarity, percentages of cases where $CompInfo$ is positive (ie., composition is informative), and both $Rec@1$ and $Rec@5$. As can be seen, all measures are significantly higher for the compositional group than for the control group both in visual and linguistic modality. Focusing on vision, the cases in which composition provides additional information compared to the closest N-constituent drops from 76.3% of the compositional group to 16.6% of the control group. Interestingly, the same trend is confirmed by Similarity and Recall measures. This confirms the intuition that for combinations involving either superimposition of an object over a background or object concatenation the composition can be obtained with a simple additive model. It also confirms that a large number of conceptual combinations cannot be composed with a simple additive model, as shown by the randomly choosen items of the control group. Evidence for a real effectiveness of the composition is also provided by the analysis of the neighbors (ie., the closest vectors) of the working cases and their constituent nouns. For example, the observed *wastebasket* is the closest neighbor of the composed *wastebasket*, but it is not even in the top 2 positions in both *waste* (*hail*, *sunshine*) and *basket*

(*cup*, *clipboard*).

By comparing vision and language, two main differences emerge. First, the average similarity in each group is significantly lower in language compared to the visual modality. That is, the composed and the observed vectors are on average closer in vision than in language[3]. Second, a different drop in the percentage of working cases can be observed between the compositional and the control group in language and vision. Whereas the percentage of working cases in the compositional group is exactly the same between the two modalities (76.3%), the performance in the linguistic control group is significantly higher than in its visual counterpart (ie., 58.3% vs 16.6%). That is, randomly choosen items are not compositional in vision, but compositional to some extent in language. Interestingly, the same percentage of working cases (76.3%) between the two modalities in the compositional group does not result from the same items. To illustrate, *bagpipe* turns out to be compositional in vision but not in language, whereas *corkscrew* is compositional in language but not in vision. Consistently with our hypothesis, *corkscrew* would require more than the grounded information provided by the visual representations of *cork* and *screw*. In contrast, summing together *bag* and *pipe* gives something similar to a *bagpipe* in vision, but not in language.

7 Conclusions

A simple additive model is effective in generating composed representations that approximate the observed representations for NN-combinations made up by either superimposed or concatenated objects. On the other hand, the same method cannot be applied to the full range of NN-compounds,

---

[3]One could think that this difference is due to the different setting used for the two modalities: the visual vectors encode one image vs. the linguistic vectors encode all the contexts in which the word is used. However, this is in not the case, since we have observed the same behavior (for the cases where compositionality works in vision) on a previous study carried out on large image datasets.

as the results on the control group reveal. This suggests that new compositional methods (perhaps capitalizing on both language and vision) are required to solve this task for all cases. In this light, we believe our dataset is a good starting point for any future investigation.

References

Artem Babenko, Anton Slesarev, Alexandr Chigorin, and Victor Lempitsky. 2014. Neural codes for image retrieval. In *Computer Vision–ECCV 2014*, pages 584–599. Springer.

Marco Baroni, Georgiana Dinu, and Germán Kruszewski. 2014. Don't count, predict! a systematic comparison of context-counting vs. context-predicting semantic vectors. In *ACL (1)*, pages 238–247.

Fintan J Costello and Mark T Keane. 2000. Efficient creativity: Constraint-guided conceptual combination. *Cognitive Science*, 24(2):299–349.

Pamela Downing. 1977. On the creation and use of English compound nouns. *Language*, 53(4):810–842.

Christina L Gagné and Edward J Shoben. 1997. Influence of thematic relations on the comprehension of modifier–noun combinations. *Journal of Experimental Psychology: Learning, Memory, and Cognition*, 23(1):71.

Christina L Gagné and Thomas L Spalding. 2006. Conceptual combination: Implications for the mental lexicon. In *The representation and processing of compound words*, chapter 7, pages 145–168. Oxford University Press Oxford, New York.

Justin Johnson, Andrej Karpathy, and Li Fei-Fei. 2015. Densecap: Fully convolutional localization networks for dense captioning. *arXiv preprint arXiv:1511.07571*.

Barbara J Juhasz, Yun-Hsuan Lai, and Michelle L Woodcock. 2014. A database of 629 English compound words: ratings of familiarity, lexeme meaning dominance, semantic transparency, age of acquisition, imageability, and sensory experience. *Behavior research methods*, pages 1–16.

Angeliki Lazaridou, Nghia The Pham, and Marco Baroni. 2015. Combining language and vision with a multimodal skip-gram model. *arXiv preprint arXiv:1501.02598*.

Judith N Levi. 1978. *The syntax and semantics of complex nominals*. Academic Press, New York.

Gary Libben. 2014. The nature of compounds: A psychocentric perspective. *Cognitive neuropsychology*, 31(1-2):8–25.

Rochelle Lieber and Pavol Štekauer, editors. 2009. *The Oxford Handbook of Compounding*. Oxford University Press, New York.

Tomas Mikolov, Kai Chen, Greg Corrado, and Jeffrey Dean. 2013. Efficient estimation of word representations in vector space. *arXiv preprint arXiv:1301.3781*.

Jeff Mitchell and Mirella Lapata. 2010. Composition in distributional models of semantics. *Cognitive science*, 34(8):1388–1429.

Dat Tien Nguyen, Angeliki Lazaridou, and Raffaella Bernardi. 2014. Coloring objects: adjective-noun visual semantic compositionality. In *Proceedings of the 25th International Conference on Computational Linguistics*, pages 112–114.

Vicente Ordonez, Wei Liu, Jia Deng, Yejin Choi, Alexander C Berg, and Tamara L Berg. 2016. Learning to name objects. *Communications of the ACM*, 59(3):108–115.

Denis Paperno and Marco Baroni. to appear. When the whole is less than the sum of its parts: How composition affects PMI values in distributional semantic vectors. Accepted for publication in Computational Linguistics.

Olga Russakovsky, Jia Deng, Hao Su, Jonathan Krause, Sanjeev Satheesh, Sean Ma, Zhiheng Huang, Andrej Karpathy, Aditya Khosla, Michael Bernstein, et al. 2015. Imagenet large scale visual recognition challenge. *International Journal of Computer Vision*, 115(3):211–252.

Karen Simonyan and Andrew Zisserman. 2014. Very deep convolutional networks for large-scale image recognition. *arXiv preprint arXiv:1409.1556*.

Andrea Vedaldi and Karel Lenc. 2015. *MatConvNet – Convolutional Neural Networks for MATLAB*. Proceeding of the ACM Int. Conf. on Multimedia.

Ivan Vendrov, Ryan Kiros, Sanja Fidler, and Raquel Urtasun. 2015. Order-embeddings of images and language. *arXiv preprint arXiv:1511.06361*.

Jianyu Wang and Alan L Yuille. 2015. Semantic part segmentation using compositional model combining shape and appearance. In *Proceedings of the IEEE Conference on Computer Vision and Pattern Recognition*, pages 1788–1797.

Edward J Wisniewski. 1996. Construal and similarity in conceptual combination. *Journal of Memory and Language*, 35(3):434–453.

Caiming Xiong, Stephen Merity, and Richard Socher. 2016. Dynamic memory networks for visual and textual question answering. *arXiv preprint arXiv:1603.01417*.

Exploring Different Preposition Sets, Models and Feature Sets in Automatic Generation of Spatial Image Descriptions

Adrian Muscat
Communications & Computer Engineering
University of Malta
Msida MSD 2080, Malta
`adrian.muscat@um.edu.mt`

Anja Belz
Computing, Engineering and Maths
University of Brighton
Lewes Road, Brighton BN2 4GJ, UK
`a.s.belz@brighton.ac.uk`

Brandon Birmingham
Communications & Computer Engineering
University of Malta
Msida MSD 2080, Malta
`brandon.birmingham.12@um.edu.mt`

Abstract

In this paper we look at the question of how to create good automatic methods for generating descriptions of spatial relationships between objects in images. In particular, we investigate the impact of varying different aspects of automatic method development, including using different preposition sets, models and feature sets. We find that optimising the preposition set improves previous best Accuracy from 46.2 to 50.2. Feature set optimisation further improves best Accuracy from 50.2 to 53.25. Naive Bayes models outperform SVMs and decision trees under all conditions tested. The utility of individual features depends on the model used, but the most useful features tend to capture a property pertaining to both objects jointly.

1 Introduction

The research reported here is located in the general area of automatic generation of image descriptions. It can be useful to generate image descriptions, either offline, e.g. to add as alt text to images in websites, or online as one aspect of assistive technology for visually impaired people.

To illustrate the specific task we address, Figure 1 shows an image from the VOC'08 data set (Everingham et al., 2010) complete with the original annotations, alongside the kind of descriptions we aim to generate: each describes the spatial relationship between two of the objects in the image in simple terms focused around a preposition.

Over the following sections, we describe the data we used, with a particular focus on the set of prepositions used in the annotations (Section 2), outline the learning methods we tested (Section 3), and report the experiments we performed and the results we obtained (Section 4).

2 Data

Our starting point is the data set we adapted previously (Belz et al., 2015) from the VOC'08 data (Everingham et al., 2010) by additionally annotating images with prepositions which describe the spatial relationships between the annotated objects in the image.

We previously used a set of 38 prepositions which were obtained in the following fashion: (a) the (complete) image descriptions collected by Rashtchian et al. (2010) for 1,000 VOC'08 (Everingham et al., 2010) images (five for each image) were parsed with the Stanford Parser version 3.5.2[1] with the PCFG model, (b) the nmod:*prep* prepositional modifier relations were extracted automatically, and (c) the non-spatial ones were removed manually. While this provided a non-arbitrary way of selecting a set of prepositions for the annotation task, it contained a large number of synonyms and near-synonyms (e.g. *in, within, inside*), which appeared to make the learning task harder (see also discussion in Section 4.2 below).

Using as a basis the frequencies and synonym sets we reported previously (Belz et al., 2015), we map this set of 38 prepositions to a reduced set, as follows. We delete from the annotations

---

[1]http://nlp.stanford.edu/software/lex-parser.shtml

Proceedings of the 5th Workshop on Vision and Language, pages 65–69,
Berlin, Germany, August 12 2016. ©2016 Association for Computational Linguistics

Figure 1: Image from VOC'08 with original annotations (left), and the kind of descriptions of spatial relationships we aim to generate automatically.

all those prepositions that were used five times or fewer by the annotators, leaving a set of 24 prepositions; next, for each synonym set, we retain only the single preposition most frequently used by the annotators, and overwrite the other members of the set with it, yielding a final set of 16 prepositions. In the following sections, we refer to the data set with the larger number of prepositions as DS-38, and the data set with the smaller number as DS-16. All results reported for DS-16 in the present paper were obtained by training models directly on this new data set.

3   Learning Methods

We use a total of four different methods: a rule-based method and a Naive Bayes model that allow direct comparison to previous work, and two new methods, namely a support vector machine (SVM) model and a decision-tree (DT) model. The latter three methods all use the feature set described in Section 4.4 below.

Rule-based method (Elliot et al.):   We use the implementation of Elliot et al.'s method we created previously (Belz et al., 2015) where handcrafted rules map a set of geometric features to the eight prepositions used by Elliot et al. (2014, p. 13).

Naive Bayes Model: We use a Naive Bayes model as in our previous work (Belz et al., 2015) which maps a set of nine handcrafted visual (including geometric) and verbal features to our set of 16 prepositions (for details of all see Section 4.4). The visual features include various measurements of object bounding box sizes, and overlap and distance between bounding boxes, while the object labels provide the language features. The model uses the language features for defining the prior

model and the visual features for defining the likelihood model.

SVM Model: Using the same features, we trained a multi-class SVM model employing one-versus-one classification.[2] This involves training $k(k-1)/2$ pairs of binary preposition classifiers for a multi-class prediction task involving k prepositions. The SVM model was trained with an RBF kernel, characterised by a coefficient of $1/(|features|)$ and set to generate the probability estimates for all classes.

Decision-Tree Model: Again using the same features, we created a multi-class decision-tree model[2] with a maximum tree depth of 4 for the DS-16 data set, and 5 for the DS-38 data set (from training and validation error plots). The model generates the probability estimates for each class.

4   Experiments

The training data contains a separate training instance (Obj_s, Obj_o, p) for each preposition p selected by human annotators for the template 'The Obj_s is p the Obj_o' (e.g. *the dog is in front of the person*) accompanied by an image in which (just) Obj_s and Obj_o are surrounded by bounding boxes. All models are trained and tested with leave-one-out cross-validation.

4.1   Evaluation methods

To compare results in this paper, we use the same variants of the basic Accuracy method as in our previous work (Belz et al., 2015). One dimension along which the variants differ is whether or not synonyms are allowed to substitute for each other. In those variants in which synonyms are allowed to

---

[2]Implemented using scikit-learn (http://scikit-learn.org).

	DS-38		DS-16	
	$Acc(1)$	$Acc^{Syn}(1)$	$Acc(1)$	$Acc^{Syn}(1)$
RB	29.8	31.6	31.4	32.0
PM	40.8	43.9	48.1	48.1
LM	28.5	36.4	32.4	32.4
NB	**46.2**	50.3	**50.2**	50.2

Table 1: $Acc(1)$ and $Acc^{Syn}(1)$ for the data with the larger (DS-38) and smaller (DS-16) preposition sets, and for the rule-based model (RB), the Naive Bayes model (NB), and the two component models of the NB model (PM and LM).

substitute for each other (Acc^{Syn}), a system output is considered correct as long as it is in the same synonym set as the target (human-selected) output. Those variants which do not take synonyms into account are referred to simply as Acc.

The second dimension along which Accuracy variants differ is output rank. Different variants (denoted $Acc(n)$ and $Acc^{Syn}(n)$) return Accuracy rates for the top n outputs, where $n = 1...4$, produced by systems, such that a system output is considered correct as long as the target (human-selected) output is among the top n outputs produced by the system.

4.2 Comparing different preposition sets

The indication from the evaluation results reported we previously (Belz et al., 2015) was that the presence of sets of synonymous prepositions in the data was adversely affecting the learning process. Note that while the *evaluations* in that work took synonyms into account, the *training phase* did not. Acc^{Syn} results in the previous work were higher than Acc results for all methods investigated, by between 2 and 6 percentage points. This indicated that higher Accuracy rates could be achieved by reducing the number of synonymous prepositions. We tested this hypothesis in our first set of experiments, reported in this section, where we directly replicate the previous experiments, but training on our new annotations which eliminate synonyms.

Table 1 has direct comparisons of the results for the two methods tested in previous work (RB = rule-based model; NB = Naive Bayes model), for the original data set with 38 prepositions (DS-38) and the new version with 16 (DS-16). Note that as in the previous work the two component parts of the Naive Bayes model are also tested separately (PM = prior model; LM = likelihood model).

As expected, the main results ($Acc(1)$ figures) are higher for DS-16 for all four models. The impact is greatest for the PM model, which is improved by just over 7 percentage points. The headline results (highlighted in bold in the table) show that the best model (NB) improves by 4 percentage points through the removal of synonyms from the training set, almost the exact extent predicted by the Acc^{Syn} results for DS-38.

4.3 Comparing different models

We tested the two previous methods (RB and NB) as well as two new models (SVM and DT) on both the DS-38 and the DS-16 data sets (for descriptions of the four models see Section 3). For the first set of experiments, we tested the four models on the two data sets using the same nine features used previously (experiments for different feature sets are reported in the following section).

The results are shown in Table 2. The Acc and Acc^{Syn} numbers show that the Naive Bayes model outperforms the rule-based baseline, the SVM and the decision tree under all conditions tested.

Looking at results for DS-38 compared to DS-16, we see that the SVM and DT models also benefit substantially from the removal of synonyms in the annotations; in fact the benefit is greatest for the SVM method (27 vs. 35.6). Informal examination of the SVM output also shows that this method is particularly sensitive to differences in preposition frequencies, tending to cluster the prepositions around the 7 or 8 highest-frequency prepositions.

4.4 Comparing different feature sets

The third aspect we investigated was the set of features being used in each method, again with a view to improving results. The results reported in previous sections above were all obtained with the same set of nine features:

$F0$: Object label L_s.

$F1$: Object label L_o.

$F2$: Area of bounding box of Obj_s normalised by image size.

$F3$: Area of bounding box of Obj_o normalised by image size.

$F4$: Ratio of area of Obj_s bounding box to that of Obj_o.

$F5$: Distance between bounding box centroids.

$F6$: Area of overlap of bounding boxes normalised by the smaller bounding box.

<table>
<tr><td colspan="5" align="center">DS-38</td><td colspan="5" align="center">DS-16</td></tr>
<tr><td></td><td colspan="4" align="center">$Acc(1..n)$</td><td></td><td colspan="4" align="center">$Acc(1..n)$</td></tr>
<tr><td>Model</td><td>$n=1$</td><td>$n=2$</td><td>$n=3$</td><td>$n=4$</td><td>Model</td><td>$n=1$</td><td>$n=2$</td><td>$n=3$</td><td>$n=4$</td></tr>
<tr><td>RB</td><td>29.8</td><td>38.7</td><td>44.5</td><td>44.6</td><td>RB</td><td>31.4</td><td>41.3</td><td>46.5</td><td>46.7</td></tr>
<tr><td>NB</td><td>46.2</td><td>60.6</td><td>69.9</td><td>77.6</td><td>NB</td><td>50.2</td><td>65.2</td><td>76.5</td><td>83.9</td></tr>
<tr><td>SVM</td><td>27.0</td><td>47.0</td><td>56.2</td><td>65.2</td><td>SVM</td><td>35.8</td><td>56.0</td><td>72.7</td><td>78.9</td></tr>
<tr><td>DT</td><td>39.3</td><td>53.4</td><td>67.2</td><td>73.7</td><td>DT</td><td>42.8</td><td>59.8</td><td>73.1</td><td>81.8</td></tr>
<tr><td></td><td colspan="4" align="center">$Acc^{Syn}(1..n)$</td><td></td><td colspan="4" align="center">$Acc^{Syn}(1..n)$</td></tr>
<tr><td></td><td>$n=1$</td><td>$n=2$</td><td>$n=3$</td><td>$n=4$</td><td></td><td>$n=1$</td><td>$n=2$</td><td>$n=3$</td><td>$n=4$</td></tr>
<tr><td>RB</td><td>31.6</td><td>40.8</td><td>46.6</td><td>46.7</td><td>RB</td><td>32.0</td><td>41.6</td><td>46.5</td><td>46.7</td></tr>
<tr><td>NB</td><td>50.3</td><td>63.9</td><td>72.2</td><td>80.0</td><td>NB</td><td>50.2</td><td>65.2</td><td>76.5</td><td>83.9</td></tr>
<tr><td>SVM</td><td>29.8</td><td>52.6</td><td>63.5</td><td>69.7</td><td>SVM</td><td>35.8</td><td>56.0</td><td>72.7</td><td>78.9</td></tr>
<tr><td>DT</td><td>41.6</td><td>56.5</td><td>71.1</td><td>76.1</td><td>DT</td><td>42.8</td><td>59.8</td><td>73.1</td><td>81.8</td></tr>
</table>

Table 2: Acc and Acc^{Syn} results for all four models (leaving out component models) described in Section 3, and the two data sets described in Section 2.

$F7$: Distance between centroids divided by the approximated average width of the two bounding boxes.

$F8$: Position of Obj_s relative to Obj_o (N, E, S, W).

Table 3 shows Accuracy rates achieved using the same experimental set-up as in previous sections, but using just single features (where this is possible[3]). The bottom row, for ease of reference, shows the Accuracy achieved when using the complete set of 9 features.

The numbers show that the different features achieve varying Accuracy rates within the context of each of the two methods. For example, it is F7 that achieves the highest Accuracy on its own in the NB method, but F8 in the DT method. It is also noticeable that, for the NB model, F4 (ratio of bounding box sizes) on its own achieves a better result than all features combined.

The above only tells us about individual features in isolation, so we also carried out greedy feature selection using the LASSO method, adding the best feature in each round (using our own implementation). The results are shown in Table 4, as applied to the DT model at the top, and the NB model in the middle. Note that because the two language features, $F0$ and $F1$, constitute the (separate) prior model component in the NB model (with the remaining features making up the likelihood model), we cannot apply LASSO to the NB model in quite the same way as for the DT model, instead initialising the feature set to $\{F0, F1\}$. For comparability, we also show results for doing the same for the DT model (lower third of Table 4).

Feature Set	$Acc(1)$		
	DT	NB init. to $\{F0, F1\}$	NB without $\{F0, F1\}$ (=LM)
$\{F0\}$	35.5	(48.1)	(48.1)
$\{F1\}$	35.6	(48.1)	(48.1)
$\{F2\}$	31.4	48.3	4.7
$\{F3\}$	31.9	47.65	12.1
$\{F4\}$	36.7	**51.05**	25.6
$\{F5\}$	33.0	47.85	12.01
$\{F6\}$	34.8	47.85	11.01
$\{F7\}$	39.5	49.45	13.5
$\{F8\}$	**40.0**	45.84	13.4
$\{F0..F8\}$	42.8	50.2	32.4

Table 3: $Acc(1)$ for each feature individually (where possible), for the smaller (DS-16) number of prepositions, for the Decision Tree and Naive Bayes models ($F0$ and $F1$ are the language features, and $F2..F8$ are the vision features).

Some commonalities emerge, e.g. $F4, F7$ and $F8$ are high-performing features that tend to be selected early, while $F6$ tends to be selected late. In all three cases, greedy feature selection reveals a maximum (highlighted in bold) before the complete set of features is reached which outperforms results achieved with all features, by a margin of between 3 and just over 7 percentage points.

The highest Accuracy achieved (53.25) is lower than accuracy rates reported in other preposition prediction research (Ramisa et al., 2015); however that work used different datasets and results varied widely between them.

5 Discussion

Through investigating the set of prepositions, the type of learning method, and the set of features used, we were able to improve previous best Accuracy results from 46.2 to 50.2 by removing synonyms and very low frequency prepositions

---

[3]For the NB model, we report two columns of results, one for the model initialised to F0 and F1, and the other for the NB model without F0 and F1, which makes it the LM model.

from the annotations. Two new learning methods, SVMs and decision-trees, did not in themselves result in improved scores. Finally, a simple approach to feature set optimisation, greedy LASSO feature selection, further improved the best Accuracy score from 50.2 to 53.25.

Not surprisingly, while feature set optimisation improves $Acc(n)$ scores for $n = 1$, it has less effect on scores for other values of n. E.g., for the optimised NB model, the four scores for $n = 1, n = 2, n = 3$, and $n = 4$ are 53.3, 66.7, 76.2, and 82.9, respectively, while for the non-optimised NB model, they are 50.2, 65.2, 76.5, and 83.9.

Out of those cases where the models do not get it right, they get it nearly right a lot of the time, as can be seen by comparing the $Acc(n)$ scores for different values of n in Table 2. In fact the margins between the $Acc(1)$ scores (proportion of times the correct result was ranked top by a model), and the scores for other values of n (proportion of times the correct result was one of the top n selected by a model) are greater for the new improved results using DS-16, as can be verified by looking at the top left and top right quarters of Table 2. This may indicate that there is room for further improvement, using more data or other learning methods. Another avenue for investigation is human evaluation of the results which would reveal how often the preposition selected by a model for a given pair of objects is in fact deemed correct by humans even though it happens to be not contained in the annotations for that image.

6 Conclusion

In this paper, we have investigated the effects of varying three different aspects of learning to generate prepositions that describe the spatial relationship between two objects in an image: the set of prepositions, the type of learning method, and the set of features. The investigations led to improvements in Accuracy results from 46.2 to 53.25. Among other findings we saw that the more useful features tended to be those that capture a property of the two objects together (such as the ratio between the sizes of their bounding boxes), and that the general usefulness of features depends on the model they are used in conjunction with.

References

Anja Belz, Adrian Muscat, Maxime Aberton, and Sami Benjelloun. 2015. Describing spatial relationships between objects in images in English and French. In *The 4th Workshop on Vision and Language (VL'15)*.

Desmond Elliott. 2014. *A Structured Representation of Images for Language Generation and Image Retrieval*. Ph.D. thesis, University of Edinburgh.

Mark Everingham, Luc Van Gool, Christopher KI Williams, John Winn, and Andrew Zisserman. 2010. The PASCAL Visual Object Classes (VOC) Challenge. *International Journal of Computer Vision*, 88(2):303–338.

Arnau Ramisa, Josiah Wang, Ying Lu, Emmanuel Dellandrea, Francesc Moreno-Noguer, and Robert Gaizauskas. 2015. Combining geometric, textual and visual features for predicting prepositions in image descriptions. In *Proceedings of the 2015 Conference on Empirical Methods in Natural Language Processing*, pages 214–220, Lisbon, Portugal, September. Association for Computational Linguistics.

Cyrus Rashtchian, Peter Young, Micah Hodosh, and Julia Hockenmaier. 2010. Collecting image annotations using Amazon's Mechanical Turk. In *Proceedings of the NAACL HLT 2010 Workshop on Creating Speech and Language Data with Amazon's Mechanical Turk*, pages 139–147. Association for Computational Linguistics.

Feature Set	$Acc(1)$
DT model	
$\{\mathbf{F8}\}$	40.04
$\{\mathbf{F7}, F8\}$	47.5
$\{\mathbf{F4}, F7, F8\}$	49.8
$\{F4, \mathbf{F5}, F7, F8\}$	49.8
$\{\mathbf{F2}, F4, F5, F7, F8\}$	49.35
$\{\mathbf{F1}, F2, F4, F5, F7, F8\}$	49.05
$\{F1, F2, F4, F5, \mathbf{F6}, F7, F8\}$	**49.95**
$\{F1, F2, \mathbf{F3}, F4, F5, F6, F7, F8\}$	49.75
$\{\mathbf{F0}, F1, F2, F3, F4, F5, F6, F7, F8\}$	42.8
NB model	
$\{F0, F1\}$	48.1
$\{F0, F1, \mathbf{F4}\}$	51.05
$\{F0, F1, F4, \mathbf{F7}\}$	51.85
$\{F0, F1, F4, F7, \mathbf{F8}\}$	**53.25**
$\{F0, F1, \mathbf{F3}, F4, F7, F8\}$	52.65
$\{F0, F1, \mathbf{F2}, F3, F4, F7, F8\}$	52.55
$\{F0, F1, F2, F3, F4, \mathbf{F5}, F7, F8\}$	50.95
$\{F0, F1, F2, F3, F4, F5, \mathbf{F6}, F7, F8\}$	50.2
DT model with feature set initialised to $\{F0, F1\}$	
$\{F0, F1\}$	44.5
$\{F0, F1, \mathbf{F7}\}$	44.14
$\{F0, F1, \mathbf{F4}, F7\}$	49.15
$\{F0, F1, \mathbf{F2}, F4, F7\}$	**49.25**
$\{F0, F1, F2, F4, \mathbf{F5}, F7\}$	**49.25**
$\{F0, F1, F2, F4, F5, F7, \mathbf{F8}\}$	49.15
$\{F0, F1, F2, \mathbf{F3}, F4, F5, F7, F8\}$	48.85
$\{F0, F1, F2, F3, F4, F5, \mathbf{F6}, F7, F8\}$	42.84

Table 4: $Acc(1)$ figures when applying LASSO greedy feature selection for DT and NB models, and for DT model with $F0$ and $F1$ fixed, for direct comparability with NB model.

Multi30K: Multilingual English-German Image Descriptions

Desmond Elliott   **Stella Frank**   **Khalil Sima'an**

ILLC, University of Amsterdam

d.elliott@uva.nl   s.c.frank@uva.nl   k.simaan@uva.nl

Lucia Specia

University of Sheffield

l.specia@sheffield.ac.uk

Abstract

We introduce the **Multi30K** dataset to stimulate multilingual multimodal research. Recent advances in image description have been demonstrated on English-language datasets almost exclusively, but image description should not be limited to English. This dataset extends the Flickr30K dataset with i) German translations created by professional translators over a subset of the English descriptions, and ii) German descriptions crowdsourced independently of the original English descriptions. We describe the data and outline how it can be used for multilingual image description and multimodal machine translation, but we anticipate the data will be useful for a broader range of tasks.

1 Introduction

Image description is one of the core challenges at the intersection of Natural Language Processing (NLP) and Computer Vision (CV) (Bernardi et al., 2016). This task has only received attention in a monolingual English setting, helped by the availability of English datasets, e.g. Flickr8K (Hodosh et al., 2013), Flickr30K (Young et al., 2014), and MS COCO (Chen et al., 2015). However, the possible applications of image description are useful for all languages, such as searching for images using natural language, or providing alternative-description text for visually impaired Web users.

We introduce a large-scale dataset of images paired with sentences in English and German as an initial step towards studying the value and the characteristics of multilingual-multimodal data[1].

---

[1]The dataset is freely available under the Creative Commons Attribution NonCommercial ShareAlike 4.0 International license from http://www.statmt.org/wmt16/multimodal-task.html.

Multi30K is an extension of the Flickr30K dataset (Young et al., 2014) with 31,014 German *translations* of English descriptions and 155,070 independently collected German descriptions. The translations were collected from professionally contracted translators, whereas the descriptions were collected from untrained crowdworkers. The key difference between these corpora is the relationship between the sentences in different languages. In the translated corpus, we know there is a strong correspondence between the sentences in both languages. In the descriptions corpus, we only know that the sentences, regardless of the language, are supposed to describe the same image.

A dataset of images paired with sentences in multiple languages broadens the scope of multimodal NLP research. Image description with *multilingual* data can also be seen as machine translation in a *multimodal* context. This opens up new avenues for researchers in machine translation (Koehn et al., 2003; Chiang, 2005; Sutskever et al., 2014; Bahdanau et al., 2015, *inter-alia*) to work with multilingual multimodal data. Image–sentence ranking using monolingual multimodal datasets (Hodosh et al., 2013, *inter-alia*) is also a natural task for multilingual modelling.

The only existing datasets of images paired with multilingual sentences were created by professionally translating English into the target language: IAPR-TC12 with 20,000 English-German described images (Grubinger et al., 2006), and the Pascal Sentences Dataset of 1,000 Japanese-English described images (Funaki and Nakayama, 2015). **Multi30K** dataset is larger than both of these and contains both independent and translated sentences. We hope this dataset will be of broad interest across NLP and CV research and anticipate that these communities will put the data to use in a broader range of tasks than we can foresee.

Proceedings of the 5th Workshop on Vision and Language, pages 70–74,
Berlin, Germany, August 12 2016. ©2016 Association for Computational Linguistics

1. Brick layers constructing a wall.

2. Maurer bauen eine Wand.

1. The two men on the scaffolding are helping to build a red brick wall.

2. Zwei Mauerer mauern ein Haus zusammen.

1. Trendy girl talking on her cellphone while gliding slowly down the street

2. Ein schickes Mädchen spricht mit dem Handy während sie langsam die Straße entlangschwebt.

1. There is a young girl on her cellphone while skating.

2. Eine Frau im blauen Shirt telefoniert beim Rollschuhfahren.

(a) Translations

(b) Independent descriptions

Figure 1: Multilingual examples in the **Multi30K** dataset. The independent sentences are all accurate descriptions of the image but do not contain the same details in both languages, such as shirt colour or the scaffolding. In the second translation pair (bottom left) the translator has translated "glide" as "schweben" ("to float") probably due to not seeing the image context (see Section 2.1 for more details).

2   The Multi30K Dataset

The Flickr30K Dataset contains 31,014 images sourced from online photo-sharing websites (Young et al., 2014). Each image is paired with five English descriptions, which were collected from Amazon Mechanical Turk[2]. The dataset contains 145,000 training, 5,070 development, and 5,000 test descriptions. The **Multi30K** dataset extends the Flickr30K dataset with *translated* and *independent* German sentences.

2.1   Translations

The translations were collected from professional English-German translators contracted via an established Language Service in Germany. Figure 1 presents an example of the differences between the types of data. We collected one translated description per image, resulting in a total of 31,014 translations. To ensure an even distribution over description length, the English descriptions were chosen based on their relative length, with an equal number of longest, shortest, and median length source descriptions. We paid a total of €23,000 to collect the data (€0.06 per word). Translators were shown an English language sentences and asked to produce a correct and fluent translation for it in German, without seeing the image. We decided against showing the images to translators to make this process as close as possible to a standard translation task, also making the data collected here distinct from the independent

descriptions collected as described in Section 2.2.

2.2   Independent Descriptions

The descriptions were collected from crowdworkers via the Crowdflower platform[3]. We collected five descriptions per image in the Flickr30K dataset, resulting in a total of 155,070 sentences. Workers were presented with a translated version of the data collection interface used by (Hodosh et al., 2013), as shown in Figure 2. We translated the interface to make the task as similar as possible to the crowdsourcing of the English sentences. The instructions were translated by one of the authors and checked by a native German Ph.D student.

185 crowdworkers took part in the task over a period of 31 days. We split the task into 1,000 randomly selected images per day to control the quality of the data and to prevent worker fatigue. Workers were required to have a German-language skill certification and be at least a Crowdflower Level 2 Worker: they have participated in at least 10 different Crowdflower jobs, have passed at least 100 quality-control questions, and have an job acceptance rate of at least 85%.

The descriptions were collected in batches of five images per job. Each image was randomly selected from the complete set of 1,000 images for that day, and workers were limited to writing at most 250 descriptions per day. We paid workers $0.05 per description[4] and prevented them from

---

[2]http://www.mturk.com

[3]http://www.crowdflower.com

[4]This is the same rate as Rashtchian et al. (2010) and El-

Figure 2: The German instructions shown to crowdworkers were translated from the original instructions.

submitting faster than 90 seconds per job to discourage poor/low-quality work. This works out at a rate of 40 jobs per hour, i.e. 200 descriptions per hour. We configured Crowdflower to automatically ban users who worked faster than this rate. Thus the theoretical maximum wage per hour was $10/hour. We paid a total of $9,591.24 towards collecting the data and paying the Crowdflower platform fees.

During the collection of the data, we assessed the quality both by manually checking a subset of the descriptions and also with automated checks. We inspected the submissions of users who wrote sentences with less than five words, and users with high type to token ratios (to detect repetition). We also used a character-level 6-gram LM to flag descriptions with high perplexity, which was very effective at catching nonsensical sentences. In general we did not have to ban or reject many users and overall description quality was high.

2.3 Translated vs. Independent Descriptions

We now analyse the differences between the translated and the description corpora. For this analysis, all sentences were stripped of punctuation and truecased using the Moses `truecaser.pl`[5] script trained over Europarl v7 and News Commentary v11 English-German parallel corpora.

Table 1 shows the differences between the corpora. The German translations are longer than the independent descriptions (11.1 vs. 9.6 words), while the English descriptions selected for trans-

lation are slightly shorter, on average, than the Flickr30k average (11.9 vs. 12.3). When we compare the German translation dataset against an equal number of sentences from the German descriptions dataset, we find that the translations also have more word types (19.3K vs. 17.6K), and more singleton types occurring only once (11.3K vs. 10.2K; in both datasets singletons comprise 58% of the vocabulary). The translations thus have a wider vocabulary, despite being generated by a smaller number of authors. The English datasets (all descriptions vs. those selected for translation) show a similar trend, indicating that these differences may be a result of the decision to select similar numbers of short, medium, and long English sentences for translation.

2.4 English vs. German

The English image descriptions are generally longer than the German descriptions, both in terms of number of words and characters. Note that the difference is much less smaller when measuring characters: German uses 22% fewer words but only 2.5% fewer characters. However, we observe a different pattern in the translation corpora: German uses 6.6% fewer words than English but 17.1% more characters. The vocabulary of the German description and translation corpora are more than twice as large as the English corpora. Additionally, the German corpora have two-to-three times as many singletons. This is likely due to richer morphological variation in German, as well as word compounding.

---

liott and Keller (2013) paid to collect English sentences.

[5] `https://github.com/moses-smt/mosesdecoder/blob/master/scripts/recaser/truecase.perl`

	Sentences	Tokens	Types	Characters	Avg. length	Singletons
Translations						
English	31,014	357,172	11,420	1,472,251	11.9	5,073
German		333,833	19,397	1,774,234	11.1	11,285
Descriptions						
English	155,070	1,841,159	22,815	7,611,033	12.3	9,230
German		1,434,998	46,138	7,418,572	9.6	26,510

Table 1: Corpus-level statistics about the translation and the description data.

3 Discussion

The **Multi30K** dataset is immediately suitable for research on a wide range of tasks, including but not limited to automatic image description, image–sentence ranking, multimodal and multilingual semantics, and machine translation. In what follows we highlight two applications in which **Multi30K** could be directly used. For more examples of approaches targeting these applications, we refer the reader to the forthcoming report on the WMT16 shared task on *Multimodal Machine Translation and Crosslingual Image Description* (Specia et al., 2016).

3.1 Multi30K for Image Description

Deep neural networks for image description typically integrate visual features into a recurrent neural network language model (Vinyals et al., 2015; Xu et al., 2015, *inter-alia*). Elliott et al. (2015) demonstrated how to build multilingual image description models that learn and transfer features between monolingual image description models. They performed a series of experiments on the IAPR-TC12 dataset (Grubinger et al., 2006) of images aligned with German translations, showing that both English and German image description could be improved by transferring features from a multimodal neural language model trained to generate descriptions in the other language. The **Multi30K** dataset will enable further research in this direction, allowing researchers to work with larger datasets with multiple references per image.

3.2 Multi30K for Machine Translation

Machine translation is typically performed using only textual data, for example news data, the Europarl corpora, or corpora harvested from the Web (CommonCrawl, Wikipedia, etc.). The **Multi30K** dataset makes it possible to further develop machine translation in a setting where multimodal data, such as images or video, are observed alongside text. The potential advantages of using multimodal information for machine translation include the ability to better deal with ambiguous source text and to avoid (untranslated) out-of-vocabulary words in the target language (Calixto et al., 2012). Hitschler and Riezler (2016) have demonstrated the potential of multimodal features in a targetside translation reranking model. Their approach is initially trained over large text-only translation copora and then fine-tuned with a small amount of in-domain data, such as our dataset. We expect a variety of translation models can be adapted to take advantage of multimodal data as features in a translation model or as feature vectors in neural machine translation models.

4 Conclusions

We introduced **Multi30K**: a large-scale multilingual multimodal dataset for interdisciplinary machine learning research. Our dataset is an extension of the popular Flickr30K dataset with descriptions and professional translations in German.

The descriptions were collected from a crowdsourcing platform, while the translations were collected from professionally contracted translators. These differences are deliberate and part of the larger scope of studying multilingual multimodal data in different contexts. The descriptions were collected as similarly as possible to the original Flickr30K dataset by translating the instructions used by Young et al. (2014) into German. The translations were collected without showing the images to the translators to keep the process as close to a standard translation task as possible.

There are substantial differences between the translated and the description datasets. The translations contain approximately the same number of tokens and have sentences of approximately the same length in both languages. These properties make them suited to machine translations models. The description datasets are very different in terms of average sentence lengths and the number of word types per language. This is likely to cause different engineering and scientific challenges because the descriptions are independently collected corpora instead of a sentence-level aligned corpus.

In the future, we want to study multilingual multimodality over a wider range of languages, for example beyond Indo-European families. We call on the community to engage with us on creating massively multilingual multimodal datasets.

Acknowledgements

DE and KS were supported by the NWO Vici grant nr. 277-89-002. SF was supported by European Union's Horizon 2020 research and innovation programme under grant agreement nr. 645452. We are grateful to Philip Schulz for checking the German translation of the worker instructions, and to Joachim Daiber for providing the pre-trained true-casing models.

References

Dzmitry Bahdanau, Kyunghyun Cho, and Yoshua Bengio. 2015. Neural machine translation by jointly learning to align and translate. In *ICLR*.

Raffaella Bernardi, Ruken Cakici, Desmond Elliott, Aykut Erdem, Erkut Erdem, Nazli Ikizler-Cinbis, Frank Keller, Adrian Muscat, and Barbara Plank. 2016. Automatic description generation from images: A survey of models, datasets, and evaluation measures. *Journal of Artificial Intelligence Research*, 55:409–442.

Iacer Calixto, Teo E. de Campos, and Lucia Specia. 2012. Images as context in statistical machine translation. In *Second Annual Meeting of the EPSRC Network on Vision & Language*.

Xinlei Chen, Hao Fang, Tsung-Yi Lin, Ramakrishna Vedantam, Saurabh Gupta, Piotr Dollár, and C. Lawrence Zitnick. 2015. Microsoft COCO captions: Data collection and evaluation server. *CoRR*, abs/1504.00325.

David Chiang. 2005. A hierarchical phrase-based model for statistical machine translation. In *ACL*, pages 263–270.

Desmond Elliott and Frank Keller. 2013. Image Description using Visual Dependency Representations. In *EMNLP*, pages 1292–1302.

Desmond Elliott, Stella Frank, and Eva Hasler. 2015. Multi-language image description with neural sequence models. *CoRR*, abs/1510.04709.

Ruka Funaki and Hideki Nakayama. 2015. Image-mediated learning for zero-shot cross-lingual document retrieval. In *EMNLP*, pages 585–590.

Michael Grubinger, Paul D. Clough, Henning Muller, and Thomas Desealers. 2006. The IAPR TC-12 benchmark: A new evaluation resource for visual information systems. In *LREC*.

Julian Hitschler and Stefan Riezler. 2016. Multimodal pivots for image caption translation. *CoRR*, abs/1601.03916.

Micah Hodosh, Peter Young, and Julia Hockenmaier. 2013. Framing Image Description as a Ranking Task: Data, Models and Evaluation Metrics. *Journal of Artificial Intelligence Research*, 47:853–899.

Philipp Koehn, Franz Josef Och, and Daniel Marcu. 2003. Statistical phrase-based translation. In *NAACL*, pages 48–54.

Cyrus Rashtchian, Peter Young, Micha Hodosh, and Julia Hockenmaier. 2010. Collecting image annotations using Amazon's Mechanical Turk. In *NAACL-HLT Workshop on Creating Speech and Language Data with Amazon's Mechanical Turk*.

Lucia Specia, Stella Frank, Khalil Sima'an, and Desmond Elliott. 2016. A shared task on multimodal machine translation and crosslingual image description. In *First Conference on Machine Translation*.

Ilya Sutskever, Oriol Vinyals, and Quoc V. V Le. 2014. Sequence to sequence learning with neural networks. In *Advances in Neural Information Processing Systems 27*, pages 3104–3112. Curran Associates, Inc.

Oriol Vinyals, Alexander Toshev, Samy Bengio, and Dumitru Erhan. 2015. Show and tell: A neural image caption generator. In *CVPR*.

Kelvin Xu, Jimmy Ba, Ryan Kiros, Kyunghyun Cho, Aaron C. Courville, Ruslan Salakhutdinov, Richard S. Zemel, and Yoshua Bengio. 2015. Show, attend and tell: Neural image caption generation with visual attention. *CoRR*, abs/1502.03044.

Peter Young, Alice Lai, Micha Hodosh, and Julia Hockenmaier. 2014. From image descriptions to visual denotations: New similarity metrics for semantic inference over event descriptions. *Transactions of the Association for Computational Linguistics*.

"Look, some green circles!": Learning to quantify from images [*]

Ionut Sorodoc and **Angeliki Lazaridou** and **Gemma Boleda**
Aurélie Herbelot and **Sandro Pezzelle** and **Raffaella Bernardi**
CIMeC - Center for Mind/Brain Sciences, University of Trento
`first.lastname@unitn.it`

Abstract

In this paper, we investigate whether a neural network model can learn the meaning of natural language quantifiers (*no, some* and *all*) from their use in visual contexts. We show that memory networks perform well in this task, and that explicit counting is not necessary to the system's performance, supporting psycholinguistic evidence on the acquisition of quantifiers.

1 Introduction

Multimodal representations of meaning have recently gained a lot of attention in the computational semantics literature. It has been shown, in particular, that the meaning of content words can be modelled in a cognitively – and even neuroscientifically – plausible way by learning representations from both the linguistic and visual contexts in which a lexical item has been observed (Anderson et al., 2013; Lazaridou et al., 2015). Such work has been crucial to advance the development of both a) a computational theory of meaning rooted in situated language use, as pursued by the field of Distributional Semantics (Clark, 2012; Erk, 2012) and b) vision-based applications such as image caption generation and visual question answering (Antol et al., 2015), going towards genuine image understanding.

Both distributional semantics and visual applications, however, struggle with providing plausible representations for function words. This has theoretical and practical consequences. On the theoretical side, it simply reduces the explanatory power of the model, in particular with respect to accounting for the compositionality of language. On the practical side, current vision systems are forced to rely on background language models instead of truly interpreting the words of a query or caption in the given visual context. As a consequence, if e.g. the sentence *I see some cats* is more frequent than *I see no cat*, language model-based applications will tend to generate the first even when the second would be more appropriate.

In this paper, we start remedying this situation by investigating one important class of function words: natural language quantifiers (e.g. *no, some, all*). Quantifiers are an emerging field of research in distributional semantics (Grefenstette, 2013; Herbelot and Vecchi, 2015) and, so far, haven't been studied in relation with visual data and grounding. We make a first step in this direction by asking whether the meaning of quantifier words can be learnt by observing their use in the presence of visual information. We observe that in grounded contexts, children learn to make quantification estimates before being able to count (Feigenson et al., 2004; Mazzocco et al., 2011), using their Approximate Number Sense (ANS). We ask whether Neural Networks (NNs) can model this ability, and we evaluate several neural network models, with and without numerical processing ability, on the task of matching a non-cardinal to a referent in a grounded situation.

NNs have been shown to perform well in tasks related to quantification, from counting to simulating the ANS. Seguí et al. (2015), for instance, explore the task of counting occurrences of an object in an image using convolutional NNs, and demonstrate that object identification can be learnt as a surrogate of counting. Stoianov and Zorzi (2012) show that the ANS emerges as a statistical property of images in deep networks that learn a hi-

---

[*]This project has received funding from the European Unions Horizon 2020 research and innovation programme under the Marie Sklodowska-Curie grant agreement No 655577 (LOVe); ERC 2011 Starting Independent Research Grant n. 283554 (COMPOSES). We gratefully acknowledge the support of NVIDIA Corporation with the donation of the GPUs used in our research.

Proceedings of the 5th Workshop on Vision and Language, pages 75–79,
Berlin, Germany, August 12 2016. ©2016 Association for Computational Linguistics

erarchical generative model of visual input. To our knowledge, however, there hasn't been any attempt so far to model the use of non-cardinals (*no, some, all*) in a visual quantification task.

Our paper builds on previous work by proposing a NN model of quantifier terms which can be related to the acquisition of the ANS, with two main contributions: First, we propose a novel experimental setup in which, given a set of objects with different properties (e.g., circles of different colors), the model learns to apply the correct quantifier to the situation (e.g. *no, some, all* circles are red). Second, we show that, as observed in children, our best model does not need to be able to count in order to quantify.[1]

2 Visual Quantification Dataset

Linguistic quantifiers and their logical properties have been a major object of study in the field of formal semantics since its inception (Montague, 1974). It is posited that, in an example such as *some circles are green*, the quantifier (*some*) expresses a relation between a domain restrictor (*circles*) and the quantifier's scope (*are green*). In this paper, we fix the domain and focus on the scope: We ask whether, given an image with objects from a single domain (circles), a model can learn to globally quantify the objects with a certain property, deciding whether *all*, *some*, or *no* circles have that property. Here, we use color as an example property to quantify over.

Images. In order to focus on the quantification task, barring out any effect from data preprocessing, we create an artificial dataset with clear visual properties (see below). Our dataset consists of images with 1 to 16 circles of 15 different colors, and we generate all possible combinations of different numbers of circles (from 1 to 16) with all possible combinations of colors. Figure 1 presents one of the images in the dataset.

Image representation. In order to avoid effects from visual pre-processing, the dataset is presented to the quantification network with (automatically produced) gold standard information about image segmentation and object identification. That is, the network knows *where* objects are, and *what* they are (circles of different, easily identifiable colors). Concretely, we represent each picture as a set of up to 16 circles (e.g. Fig-

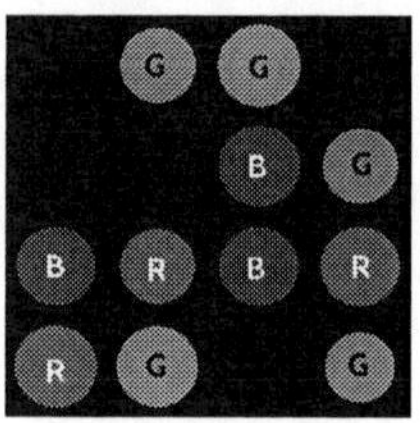

Figure 1: One of the images in our visual quantification dataset. Letters indicate color: R(ed), G(reen), B(lue).

ure 1) placed in 16 fixed image cells. Furthermore, we associate each of the circle-color combination with real-valued vectors of dimensionality 20 that are normalized to unit norm. All circles are identical in shape and size, so the differences observable in the vector representations can be taken to express the color property of the objects. We ensure that the dataset does not include 'confusable' objects by further constraining the vectors to have low pairwise similarity.[2] On the other hand, to prevent overfitting, we add a small amount of noise to all vectors, generated for each dimension from a Gaussian distribution with mean 0 and variance 1/5 of the original variance of that dimension. Intuitively, the Gaussian noise simulates natural variations in a given property, e.g., two tennis balls being of slightly different shades of yellow. This is applied to both training and test data. Finally, our images may contain *empty cells*, viz. parts of the image with no object in it (e.g., in Figure 1 there are 5 empty cells.) These are similarly represented by a vector, randomly generated so that it be orthogonal to all the other object vectors.

Queries Each image in the dataset is associated with a *query*, i.e., the property we want to quantify over, and the task of the model is to associate the correct *quantifier* with the query for the image. For instance, the query associated to the image in Figure 1 is *green* and the correct quantifier is *some*. *Some* encodes "at least one but not all circles have color X", *all* encodes "all circles have color X" and *no* "no circle has color X". Our dataset contains 5K <image, query, quantifier> datapoints split equally amongst the three quantifiers,[3] which will be used to evaluate our models.

---

[2]We fix this parameter to values not exceeding a cosine similarity of 0.7

[3]Note that, although the *all* quantifier generates fewer images than *no* and *some*, it is possible to create balanced data by producing noisy variations of a same image.

3 Models

Our aim is to understand whether NNs can learn to quantify objects of a certain property in a given image. Our main hypothesis in this paper is that for acquiring such ability the model does not need to rely on exact number information but it can do so by computing the gist of the queried property in the image, thus simulating the human ANS. We build three models to test this hypothesis.

Quantification Memory Network (qMN): This is the model we propose in this paper; it is designed to show that knowing how to count is not a *necessary* condition to be able to learn to quantify. It is an adaptation of the memory network of Sukhbaatar et al. (2015) for visual quantification. As shown in Figure 2, the model consists of a memory with 16 slots, one for each image cell. It computes the dot product between each memory slot and the vector query, obtaining 16 scores, which are then fed into a softmax classifier to derive a valid probability distribution. These normalized scores are used to derive the "gist" of the image (a 20-D vector), by computing a weighted sum over cell vectors in the memory slots, where the weights are taken from the probability distribution that is output by the softmax classifier. Finally, a non-linear transformation with a ReLU activation is applied over the concatenation of the "gist" and query vectors. The vector dimensionality is reduced to 3 by linear transformation and a softmax classifier is applied on top of that, deriving a probability distribution over the three quantifiers. The "gist" vector is an aggregate of the memory, and information about individual objects is lost, such that the model is not able to count. However, the similarity between the "gist" and the query reflects the ratio (rather than the exact number) of objects of that color in the image. To make this explicit, in the case of 'all' , the gist and query vectors will be almost identical, in the case of 'no' there will hardly be any trace of the query in the gist, making them different, and in the case of 'some' query and gist will be somewhat similar.

Counting model: We note that a simple rule-based model comparing the cardinalities of the restrictor and scope in the query would achieve 100% accuracy. But we want to check to what extent a NN model based on softmax and non-linear transformation, similar to qMN, can learn to quantify when provided with *exact number information* about the objects and their colors. Indeed,

despite the obvious logical interpretation of quantifiers as ratios between two magnitudes, it is unclear whether this logical operation is easily learnable in a visual connectionist model. In this setup, we build for each image a 16-D feature vector, one dimension for each of the 15 colors plus one for the empty cell. To each dimension we assign a value encoding the frequency of the color in the image scaled by the similarity of that color to the query (recall that, because of the added Gaussian noise, a given yellow circle may not be identical to the query *yellow*). This way, the quantity of objects of a given color is encoded in the dimensions of the vector as if the model was counting. The query is represented by a one-hot 16-D vector, encoding the color the model is asked to quantify over. The feature and query vectors are concatenated. As in the qMN model, we then apply a linear transformation followed by a ReLU activation and a softmax classifier.

Recurrent Neural Network (RNN): As an alternative model with a visual memory, we also implement an RNN that uses the hidden state to encode information about the image's gist. At each timestep, the RNN receives as input first the query vector followed by each of the 16 objects vectors. At the last timestep, the hidden layer is fed to a linear transformation, reducing its size to 3, on top of which a softmax classifier is applied to obtain a probability distribution over the quantifiers. As opposed to the qMN, the RNN does not explicitly model the similarity between the query and the color of the objects in the image.

All models are trained with cross-entropy to predict the correct quantifier.

4 Experimental setup

We randomly divide the 5K data points into training, validation and test set (70%, 10% and 20%). We test the models in 3 experimental setups. The first setup, **familiar**, is the simplest, and tests whether models are able to quantify previously observed ("familiar") colors and quantities. In the **unseen quantities** setup, we create training and test sets so that there is no overlap with respect to the number of objects in the image: 4, 9 or 13 objects are used at test time and all other quantities at training/validation time (i.e., 1-3, 5-8, 10-12, 14-16). Finally, in the **unseen colors** setup, we make sure training and test sets differ with respect to objects' color: The models are trained/validated on

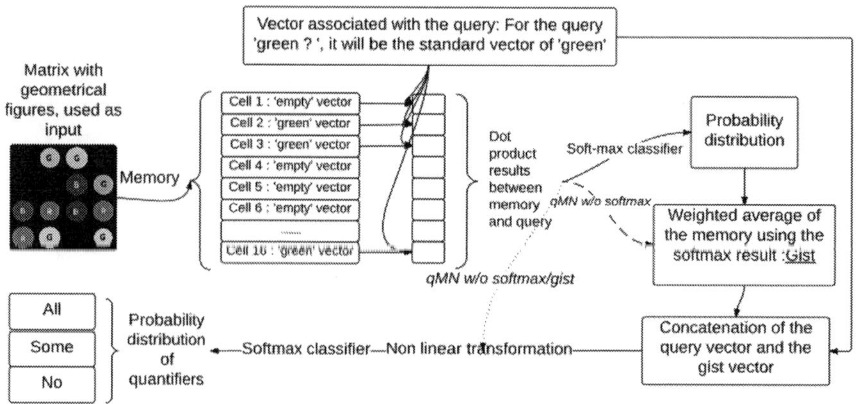

Figure 2: Quantification Memory Network model

Models	familiar	unseen quantities	unseen colors
RNN	65.7	62.0	49.7
Counting	86.5	78.4	32.8
qMN	**88.8**	**97.0**	**54.9**
-softmax	85.9	66.6	54.4
-softmax/gist	51.4	51.8	44.4

Table 1: Model accuracies (in %).

10 colors and tested on 5 additional, unseen colors. We expect that the use of the gist in our model, which implements *global* quantification over objects of a certain property, will allow it to generalize well when tested against unseen quantities.

5 Results

As shown in Table 1, having exact number information is not necessary for learning to quantify: The qMN model, which does not explicitly count, is more accurate than the Counting model in all test conditions. Even though both models outperform the RNN model when tested on unseen number of objects, only the qMN model truly generalizes the learnt quantification operation. The performance of all models drops when tested on unseen colors, though qMN still performs best and the decrease in performance in Counting is much worse than in the qMN model (-53.7 vs. -34). Lines "-softmax" and "-softmax/gist" in Table 1 show that both the softmax and the "gist" are crucial elements of the model; removing them causes significant performance drops in all test conditions.

By looking at the confusion matrices for the qMN model we observe that there is generally more confusion between *no* and *some* than in pairs involving *all*; the gist for *some* is an average of potentially several different colors, and thus less straightforwardly interpretable. In the 'familiar' test, most of the errors come from situations in which the model confused "some" with "no" *and* the image contains just 1 or at most 2 occurrences of the queried color. Hence, the increase in performance from the familiar to the unseen quantity test (+8.2) is due to the absence of very small cardinalities in the image (the lowest is 4 items.) As for *all*, in both the 'familiar' and the 'unseen quantities' conditions it's nearly always classified correctly. This is to be expected because in this case, the "gist" computation produces a vector which should be cleanly equivalent to the query (minus the effect of noise). When moving to unseen properties performance decreases, indicating that the network might have overfitted to the particular colors in the training set. Although we'll need to address this behaviour in further work, we don't consider it a weakness of a *quantification* model per se: the problem to be solved is one of object/property recognition and not of quantification.

6 Conclusion

We have shown that a memory network can learn to quantify objects of a certain property, given some visually grounded training data involving small sets. Given that the number of memory cells is parametric, the model should in principle be able to scale to much larger number of cells. Our future work will focus on modelling the entire quantifier meaning, varying not only the quantifier scope but also its *restriction*.

References

Andrew J Anderson, Elia Bruni, Ulisse Bordignon, Massimo Poesio, and Marco Baroni. 2013. Of words, eyes and brains: Correlating image-based distributional semantic models with neural representations of concepts. In *EMNLP*, pages 1960–1970.

Stanislaw Antol, Aishwarya Agrawal, Jiasen Lu, Margaret Mitchell, Dhruv Batra, C Lawrence Zitnick, and Devi Parikh. 2015. Vqa: Visual question answering. In *Proceedings of the IEEE International Conference on Computer Vision*, pages 2425–2433.

Stephen Clark. 2012. Vector space models of lexical meaning. In Shalom Lappin and Chris Fox, editors, *Handbook of Contemporary Semantics – second edition*. Wiley-Blackwell.

Katrin Erk. 2012. Vector space models of word meaning and phrase meaning: a survey. *Language and Linguistics Compass*, 6:635–653.

Lisa Feigenson, Stanislas Dehaene, and Elizabeth Spelke. 2004. Core systems of number. *Trends in cognitive sciences*, 8(7):307–314.

Edward Grefenstette. 2013. Towards a formal distributional semantics: Simulating logical calculi with tensors. In *Proceedings of the Second Joint Conference on Lexical and Computational Semantics (STARSEM)*.

Aurélie Herbelot and Eva Maria Vecchi. 2015. Building a shared world: Mapping distributional to model-theoretic semantic spaces. In *Proceedings of the 2015 Conference on Empirical Methods in Natural Language Processing*, Lisbon, Portugal. https://www.aclweb.org/anthology/W/W13/W13-0204.pdf.

Angeliki Lazaridou, Nghia The Pham, and Marco Baroni. 2015. Combining language and vision with a multimodal skip-gram model. In *Proceedings of NAACL*.

Michèle MM Mazzocco, Lisa Feigenson, and Justin Halberda. 2011. Preschoolers' precision of the approximate number system predicts later school mathematics performance. *PLoS one*, 6(9):e23749.

Richard Montague. 1974. The proper treatment of quantification in ordinary English. In R. Thomason, editor, *Formal Philosophy*, pages 247–270. Yale University Press, New Haven.

Santi Seguí, Oriol Pujol, and Jordi Vitria. 2015. Learning to count with deep object features. In *Proceedings of the IEEE Conference on Computer Vision and Pattern Recognition Workshops*, pages 90–96.

Ivilin Stoianov and Marco Zorzi. 2012. Emergence of a 'visual number sense' in hierarchical generative models. *Nature neuroscience*, 15(2):194–196.

Sainbayar Sukhbaatar, Arthur Szlam, Jason Weston, and Rob Fergus. 2015. End-to-end memory networks. http://arxiv.org/abs/1503.08895.

Text2voronoi: An Image-driven Approach to Differential Diagnosis

Alexander Mehler
Goethe University
Institute of Computer Science
Text Technology Lab

Tolga Uslu
Goethe University
Institute of Computer Science
Text Technology Lab

Wahed Hemati
Goethe University
Institute of Computer Science
Text Technology Lab

{mehler,uslu,hemati}@em.uni-frankfurt.de

Abstract

Differential diagnosis aims at distinguishing between diseases causing similar symptoms. This is exemplified by epilepsies and dissociative disorders. Recently, it has been shown that linguistic features of physician-patient talks allow for differentiating between these two diseases. Since this method relies on trained linguists, it is not suitable for daily use. In this paper, we introduce a novel approach, called text2voronoi, for utilizing the paradigm of text visualization to reconstruct differential diagnosis as a task of text categorization. In line with current research on linguistic differential diagnosis, we explore linguistic characteristics of physician-patient talks to span our feature space. However, unlike standard approaches to categorization, we do not use linguistic feature spaces directly, but explore visual features derived from the talks' pictorial representations. That is, we provide an approach to *image-driven differential diagnosis*. By example of 24 talks of epileptics and dissociatively disordered patients, we show that our approach outperforms its counterpart based on the bag-of-words model.

1 Introduction

Physicians use medical imaging for diagnosing. Bone fractures, for example, are visualized by radiographs, pregnancies are examined by means of ultrasound scans, while neurological disorders are studied with the help of MRI scans. Our goal is to assist physicians in diagnosing mental disorders by analogy to such image-driven methods. To this end, we introduce a method for scan-

ning physician-patient talks to get pictorial representations as input of classifiers which perform the differential diagnosis. This approach is in line with recent efforts in clinical NLP to utilize computational methods for automatically analyzing medical histories (Friedman et al., 2013). It profits from recent findings showing that linguistic features provide reliable bases for differentiating between epilepsies and dissociative disorders (Gülich, 2010; Reuber et al., 2009; Opp et al., 2015). Since the latter approach relies on trained linguists for performing the feature analysis it does not allow for daily use. The present paper aims at filling this gap. It introduces a new method for visualizing linguistic data by means of images as input to classifiers which learn from their pictorial features to arrive at the desired diagnoses. The main hypothesis of our paper (as elaborated in Section 3) runs as follows: *Linguistic features of physician-patient talks can be visualized in a way that a certain range of diagnoses can be derived from analyzing pictorial features of these visualizations.* In Section 3, we introduce so called <u>Vo</u>ronoi *diagrams of <u>Te</u>xts* (VoTe) to provide such expressive visualizations. VoTes are generated by our text2voronoi algorithm as described in Section 3. Unlike the classical bag-of-words model, this approach explores bags of visual features derived from the talks' image representations in terms of VoTes. To this end, we utilize the *TextImager* which automatically extracts a wide range of linguistic information from input texts to derive representational images thereof. In Section 4, we describe an experiment, which shows that our image-driven classifier can indeed differentiate between epilepsies and dissociative disorders: its F-score outperforms its classical counterpart based on the bag-of-words model. Note that we do not claim that VoTes allow for differentiating between whatever mental diseases. Rather, we start with epilep-

Proceedings of the 5th Workshop on Vision and Language, pages 80–85,
Berlin, Germany, August 12 2016. ©2016 Association for Computational Linguistics

sies and dissociative disorders as two initial examples and will extend our approach by including related diseases in future work (cf. Section 5).

2   Related Work

Recent studies have shown that a linguistic examination of physician-patient talks based on *Conversation Analysis* (CA) (Drew et al., 2001) allows for distinguishing between epileptic and non-epileptic seizures (Reuber et al., 2009; Plug et al., 2009; Plug et al., 2010; Gülich, 2010; Opp et al., 2015). Reuber et al. (2009) describe a CA-inspired experiment where two linguists blinded to medical data attempted to predict the diagnosis on the basis of qualitative linguistic assessments. Using these assessments, the linguists predicted 17 of 20 (85%) diagnoses correctly. Opp et al. (2015) found that patients with epileptic seizures try to describe their attacks as accurate as possible, whereas patients suffering from dissociative disorders avoid detailed descriptions of their seizures. As a matter of fact, such differences are mirrored by linguistic choices. However, these and related methods (Gülich, 2010) rely on the expertise of trained linguists and are, thus, not practical in terms of daily use.

Other approaches use machine learning to predict diagnoses from therapy transcripts by means of extracted linguistic features (Howes et al., 2012a). Howes et al. (2013), for example, use topics that have been derived by means of LDA. Support vector machines operating on linguistic features have also been used to predict diagnoses (Howes et al., 2012b; DeVault et al., 2013; DeVault et al., 2014). Unlike these approaches to text categorization, which rely on the bag-of-words model or some of its descendants, we use pictorial representations of linguistic features as input for our classifier. This is done by extending the UIMA-based TextImager by means of visual scans of physician-patient talks as explained in Section 3. Alternatives to the TextImager are given by the UIMA-based frameworks cTAKES (Savova et al., 2010) and EpiDEA (Cui et al., 2012). Unlike the TextImager, both tools do not provide a visualization engine and, thus, do not fit our task of text classification based on pictorial text representations.

Note that the pictorial representations of texts as introduced here rely on so called Voronoi diagrams (de Berg et al., 2000). Voronoi dia-

Label	POS
C1	Noun
C2	Verb
C3	Preposition
C4	Adjective
C5	Adverb
C6	Temporal expression

Table 1: Parts of speech and expressions explored by text2voronoi.

Label	Category	Example
G1	Case	{nominative, accusative,..}
G2	Mood	{indicative, imperative,..}
G3	Number	{singular, plural}
G4	Person	{first, second,..}
G5	Tense	{past, present,..}
G6	Gender	{feminine, masculine,..}
G7	Degree	{positive, comparative,..}

Table 2: Categories explored by text2voronoi.

grams have already been used to represent semantic structures of lexical units (Jäger, 2006). We further develop this approach in the sense of deriving Voronoi diagrams as representations of natural language texts in general.

3   The text2voronoi Model of Texts

Our goal is to generate images from physician-patient talks whose visual features can be used by classifiers to perform the desired differential diagnosis. To this end, we provide the *text2voronoi algorithm* which computes this visualization in four steps (see Figure 1):

1. extraction of linguistic features,

2. embedding the features in vector space,

3. Voronoi tesselation of this space and

4. extraction of visual features from the tesselation.

In what follows, we describe each of these steps.

3.1   Linguistic Feature Extraction

Each input text is preprocessed by the TextImager which utilizes several NLP tools to tag a range of linguistic features per lexical token. This includes POS tags (e.g., pronouns, prepositions), grammatical categories (e.g., case, gender, number, tense) and temporal expressions (e.g., dates, temporal adverbs) – see Table 1 and 2 for all POS and their features considered in Step 1 combining to 180

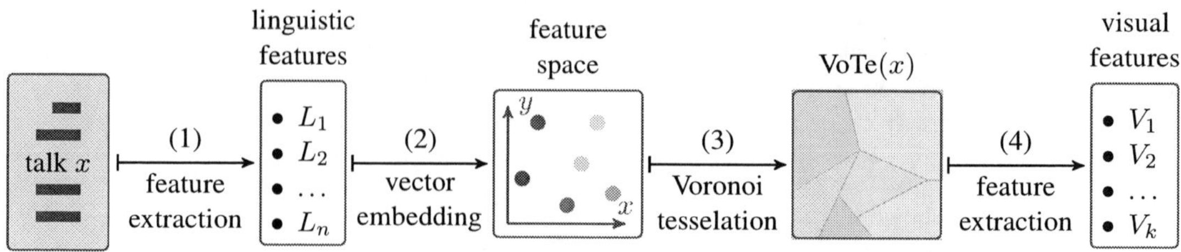

Figure 1: Workflow of the text2voronoi algorithm generating a *Voronoi diagram of* the *Text* (VoTe) x.

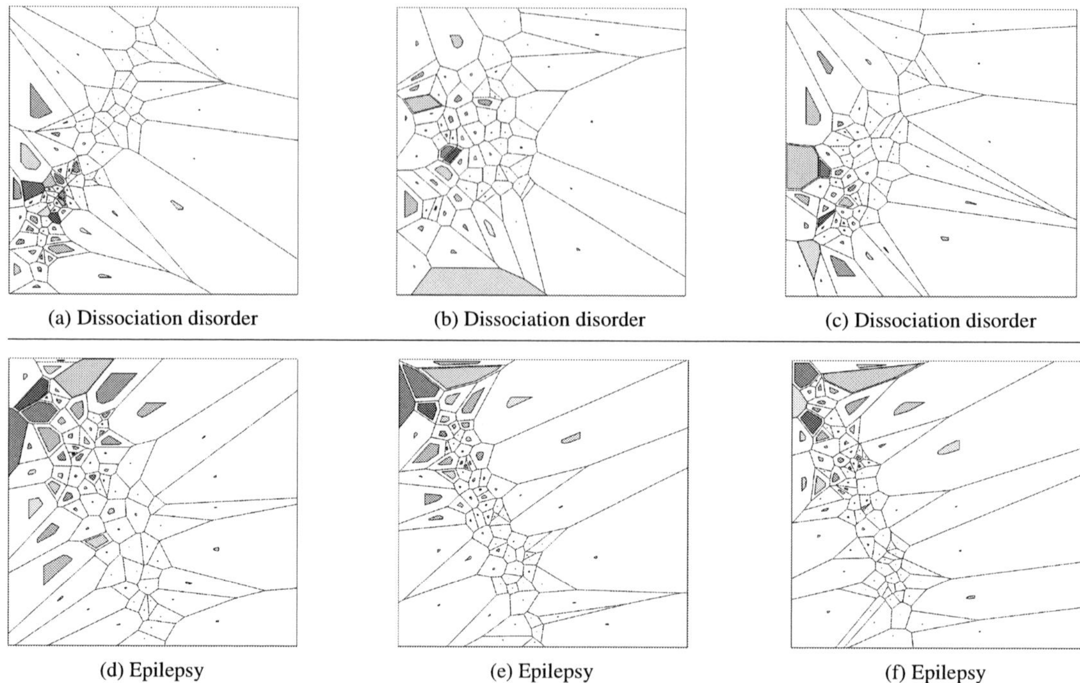

(a) Dissociation disorder   (b) Dissociation disorder   (c) Dissociation disorder

(d) Epilepsy   (e) Epilepsy   (f) Epilepsy

Figure 2: Visualizations (*VoTes*) of six physician-patient talks as used in our classification experiment.

features. The reason for selecting these features is that according to (Gülich, 2010; Opp et al., 2015), patients suffering from epilepsies tend to give detailed descriptions of their seizures, while dissociatively disordered patients tend to avoid such descriptions. Thus, while the former group of patients likely uses personal pronouns in connection with prepositions (for localizing their seizures) and polarity cues (for evaluating them), the latter group will rather avoid the co-selection of such features. For tagging POS and grammatical features, we use a retrained instance (Eger et al., 2016) of *MarMoT* (Müller et al., 2013), while *HeidelTime* (Strötgen and Gertz, 2010) is used for tagging temporal expressions.

3.2 Embedding the Features in Vector Space

Since our features are tagged per token, we can transcode each sentence of the corresponding input text as a sequence of these features to make them as input to word2vec (Mikolov et al., 2013) by projecting on exactly two dimensions. The reason behind this approach is to compute feature associations in a manner that is characteristic of the input text. Thus, we do not use a (huge) reference corpus (e.g., Wikipedia) for computing "reference" associations but explore text-*specific* patterns in our two-dimensional feature space.

3.3 Voronoi Tesselation of the Feature Space

The vector embeddings span a two-dimensional space for which we compute a Voronoi decomposition (de Berg et al., 2000). Each cell of the resulting _Voronoi diagram of_ a _Text_ (VoTe) corresponds to a single feature. Generally speaking, starting from a set P of distinct points in a plane we get a corresponding Voronoi diagram by coloring all points $q_1, \ldots$ of equal distance to at least two points in P (de Berg et al., 2000). The points $q_1, \ldots$ manifest the borders of the Voronoi regions that consist of all points with the same single nearest neighbor in P. To color the VoTe of a text, we additionally explore two kinds of frequency information: while the overall frequency of a feature determines how much of its cell is filled (starting from the center), the transparency of the cell depends on the feature's inverse sentence frequency: the smaller this value, the more transparent the cell. Figure 2 exemplifies the VoTes of 6 texts. Note that for each text each feature is mapped onto the same color in order to allow for comparing different texts. However, the exact position of a feature cell in a text's VoTe, its size, degree of filling, transparency and neighborhood depend on the specifics of that text. That is, they depend on the characteristics of the given physician-patient talk in terms of the co-occurrence statistics of the underlying linguistic features. Thus, our classification hypothesis is: _talks of patients suffering from the same disease induce similar VoTes._ Exploring the visual patterns of VoTes is then a way to perform the targeted classification.

3.4 Extracting Visual Features from VoTes

For the sake of the latter classification, we extract a set of visual features for each cell of the VoTes (see Table 3). The underlying hypothesis is that two VoTes are the more similar, the more of their equally colored cells share similar visual features. Each cell is characterized (1) by its _gestalt_ (area, corner, filling, shape, transparency), (2) _location_ (position, shape) and (3) _neighborhood_ (centrality). While the first group of features informs about how a single cell looks like, the second group informs about its localization on the map, and the third group about its relations to other cells. The more of these features are shared by two equally colored cells, the more visually similar they are. For mapping neighborhood-related features, we compute the closeness centralities of the cells in the graph representation of the Voronoi diagrams. Next, for all Voronoi cells that correspond to the 180 features of Step 1, we compute 11 features (see Table 3) so that each VoTe of a

Feature	Description	#Features
Area	The surface area	1
Position	x/y coordinates of center	2
Shape	Min (x, y), max (x, y)	4
Filling	Percentage of fill coverage	1
Transparency	Degree of opacity	1
Corner	Number of corners	1
Centrality	Closeness centrality	1

Table 3: Visual features of the cells of a Voronoi tesselation (VoTe) explored by text2voronoi.

Features	Kernel	nu-SVC	C-SVC	SVM light
All	Linear	0.832	0.832	0.832
Subset	Linear	1.0	1.0	1.0
All	RBF	0.832	0.832	0.832
Subset	RBF	0.958	1.0	1.0

Table 4: F-scores of text2voronoi-based classification.

text is finally mapped onto a vector of 1980 visual features. Note that if a linguistic feature did not occur in a talk, it was mapped onto a null vector so that VoTes get also comparable for commonly absent features.

4 Experiment

This section provides experimental data on testing the text2voronoi model. To this end, we use a German corpus of 24 physician-patient talks of 12 epileptics and 12 dissociatively disordered patients. The talks were transcribed according to GAT2 (Selting et al., 2009) and annotated w.r.t. turns and seizure descriptions (Gülich, 2010; Opp et al., 2015). The corpus was further processed according to Section 3 so that each talk was mapped onto a vector of 1980 visual features. Finally, the vectors were independently made input to _SVMlight_ and _LIBSVM_ to compute F-scores based on a leave-one-out cross-validation. Using all features, both kernels (linear and RBF) achieve an F-score of 83.2% – see Table 4. Next, we performed an optimal feature selection for SVMs (Nguyen and De la Torre, 2010) using a genetic search on our feature space with the aim of optimizing F-scores based on the same setting of cross-validation. This optimization resulted in a perfect classification (see Table 4) regardless of the kernel and the implementation of SVMs in use. Finally, we computed a bag-of-words model based on the lexical data of all talks in our corpus. Using an RBF kernel (leave-on-out cross-validation) this model

Features	Linear kernel	RBF kernel
All	0.60	0.69
Subset	0.91	0.82

Table 5: F-scores of the bag-of-words model.

achieved an F-score of 69% (see Table 5); a search for an optimal feature subset raised this score to 91% (by means of a linear kernel).

4.1 Discussion

Obviously, our findings are independent of the kernels (linear or RBF) and the SVM implementations in use. They show that by example of our corpus data, differential diagnoses come into reach based on visual depictions of the underlying talks. Moreover, we show that an optimal feature selection for SVMs can boost the classifier enormously. This may hint at problems of overfitting (negative interpretation) or at the expressiveness of the visual features in use (positive interpretation). Evidently, our corpus data is too small to decide between these alternatives. Thus, further research is required that starts from larger corpora of physician-patient talks. As a matter of fact, such data is extremely difficult to obtain (Friedman et al., 2013) so that comparative studies have to be considered in related areas of more easily accessible data. However, as indicated by our F-scores and as exemplified by Figure 2, our VoTe representations of texts are seemingly informative enough to provide visual depictions of text that may be used by physicians as scans of neurologically disordered patients based on their medical histories. Based on our results, we may speak of a novel approach to text representation according to which symbolically coded information in texts is visually reconstructed in a way that allows for performing text operations (in our case *text classification*) indirectly by processing the resulting visual representations.

5 Conclusion

We presented a novel approach to image-driven text classification based on Voronoi tesselations of linguistic features spaces. Our method allows for high score differential diagnoses by exploring features of the pictorial representations of physician-patient talks. Our experiments show that this approach outperforms classifiers based on the bag-of-words models. In order to further test its va-

lidity, we plan to experiment with larger corpora and various tasks in text classification (e.g., authorship attribution and genre detection). A major reason to do this is to clarify whether the F-scores reached by our approach so far reflect overfitting or not. To this end, we will also experiment with data of different languages. Moreover, since a great deal of information about the correct diagnosis relates to whether a patient tends to suppress the memory of her or his seizures, polarity cues are promising candidates for extending our feature space. However, since we deal with *seizure* descriptions, such a distinction is rather challenging. The reason is that turns of patients about seizures have very likely negative connotations. An alternative is to consider simpler quantitative features (turn length, number of turns etc.) to simplify the generation of VoTes. This is needed to enable automatic differential diagnoses instantaneously during physician-patient talks, which – because of error-prone speech recognition systems – require easy to measure features. Obviously, this requirement implies a trade-off: the more easily a feature is measured, the lower its semantic specificity with respect to the target classes to be learnt. Thus, a great deal of progress may be expected by developing speech recognition systems that focus on expressive linguistic features especially of physician-patient talks. Last but not least, we may consider quantitative characteristics that are more closely related to the geometry of Voronoi diagrams (e.g., in terms of their order and size – cf. (de Berg et al., 2000)). In this way, we want to contribute to the further development of text representation models based on text visualizations.

References

Licong Cui, Samden D Lhatoo, Guo-Qiang Zhang, Satya Sanket Sahoo, and Alireza Bozorgi. 2012. EpiDEA: extracting structured epilepsy and seizure information from patient discharge summaries for cohort identification. In *AMIA Annu Symp Proc.*, pages 1191–1200.

Mark de Berg, Marc van Kreveld, Mark Overmars, and Otfried Schwarzkopf. 2000. *Computational Geometry*. Springer, Berlin/Heidelberg.

David DeVault, Kallirroi Georgila, Ron Artstein, Fabrizio Morbini, David Traum, Stefan Scherer, Albert Rizzo, and Louis-Philippe Morency. 2013. Verbal indicators of psychological distress in interactive dialogue with a virtual human. In *Proc. of SIGDIAL*.

David DeVault, Ron Artstein, Grace Benn, Teresa Dey, Ed Fast, Alesia Gainer, Kallirroi Georgila, Jon Gratch, Arno Hartholt, Margaux Lhommet, Gale Lucas, Stacy Marsella, Fabrizio Morbini, Angela Nazarian, Stefan Scherer, Giota Stratou, Apar Suri, David Traum, Rachel Wood, Yuyu Xu, Albert Rizzo, and Louis-Philippe Morency. 2014. SimSensei Kiosk: A virtual human interviewer for healthcare decision support. In *Proc. of the 2014 Int. Conf. on Autonomous Agents and Multi-agent Systems (AAMAS '14)*, pages 1061–1068.

Paul Drew, John Chatwin, and Sarah Collins. 2001. Conversation analysis: a method for research into interactions between patients and health-care professionals. *Health Expectations*, 4(1):58–70.

Steffen Eger, Rüdiger Gleim, and Alexander Mehler. 2016. Lemmatization and morphological tagging in German and Latin: A comparison and a survey of the state-of-the-art. In *Proc. of LREC 2016*.

Carol Friedman, Thomas C. Rindflesch, and Milton Corn. 2013. Natural language processing: state of the art and prospects for significant progress, a workshop sponsored by the national library of medicine. *Journal of Biomedical Informatics*, 46(5):765–773.

Elisabeth Gülich. 2010. Le rôle du corpus dans l'élaboration pluridisciplinaire d'un instrument de diagnostic linguistique: l'exemple de l'épilepsie. *Pratiques. Linguistique, littérature, didactique*, (147-148):173–197.

Christine Howes, Matt Purver, Rose McCabe, Patrick GT Healey, and Mary Lavelle. 2012a. Helping the medicine go down: Repair and adherence in patient-clinician dialogues. In *Proc. of the 16th SemDial Workshop on the Semantics and Pragmatics of Dialogue (SeineDial)*.

Christine Howes, Matthew Purver, Rose McCabe, Patrick GT Healey, and Mary Lavelle. 2012b. Predicting adherence to treatment for schizophrenia from dialogue transcripts. In *Proceedings of the 13th Annual Meeting of the Special Interest Group on Discourse and Dialogue*, pages 79–83.

Christine Howes, Matthew Purver, and Rose McCabe. 2013. Using conversation topics for predicting therapy outcomes in schizophrenia. *Biomedical informatics insights*, 6(Suppl 1):39.

Gerhard Jäger. 2006. Convex meanings and evolutionary stability. In Angelo Cangelosi, Andrew D. M. Smith, and Kenny Smith, editors, *The Evolution of Language. Proc. of the 6th International Conference (EVOLANG6)*, pages 139–144, Rome.

Tomas Mikolov, Ilya Sutskever, Kai Chen, Greg S Corrado, and Jeff Dean. 2013. Distributed representations of words and phrases and their compositionality. In *Advances in Neural Information Processing Systems 26*, pages 3111–3119.

Thomas Müller, Helmut Schmid, and Hinrich Schütze. 2013. Efficient higher-order CRFs for morphological tagging. In *Proc. of the 2013 Conference on Empirical Methods in Natural Language Processing*, pages 322–332.

Minh Hoai Nguyen and Fernando De la Torre. 2010. Optimal feature selection for support vector machines. *Pattern recognition*, 43(3):584–591.

Joachim Opp, Barbara Job, and Heike Knerich. 2015. Linguistische Analyse von Anfallsschilderungen zur Unterscheidung epileptischer und dissoziativer Anfälle. *Neuropädiatrie in Klinik und Praxis*, 14(1).

Leendert Plug, Basil Sharrack, and Markus Reuber. 2009. Seizure metaphors differ in patients accounts of epileptic and psychogenic nonepileptic seizures. *Epilepsia*, 50(5):994–1000.

Leendert Plug, Basil Sharrack, and Markus Reuber. 2010. Seizure, fit or attack? The use of diagnostic labels by patients with epileptic or non-epileptic seizures. *Applied Linguistics*, 31(1):94–114.

Markus Reuber, Chiara Monzoni, Basil Sharrack, and Leendert Plug. 2009. Using interactional and linguistic analysis to distinguish between epileptic and psychogenic nonepileptic seizures: A prospective, blinded multirater study. *Epilepsy and Behavior*, 16(1):139–144.

Guergana K Savova, James J Masanz, Philip V Ogren, Jiaping Zheng, Sunghwan Sohn, Karin C Kipper-Schuler, and Christopher G Chute. 2010. Mayo clinical text analysis and knowledge extraction system (cTAKES): architecture, component evaluation and applications. *Journal of the American Medical Informatics Association*, 17(5):507–513.

Margret Selting, Peter Auer, Dagmar Barth-Weingarten, Jörg Bergmann, Pia Bergmann, Karin Birkner, Elizabeth Couper-Kuhlen, Arnulf Deppermann, Peter Gilles, Susanne Günthner, Martin Hartung, Friederike Kern, Christine Mertzlufft, Christian Meyer, Miriam Morek, Frank Oberzaucher, Jörg Peters, Uta Quasthoff, Wilfried Schütte, Anja Stukenbrock, and Susanne Uhmann. 2009. Gesprächsanalytisches Transkriptionssystem 2 (GAT 2). *Gesprächsforschung: Online-Zeitschrift zur verbalen Interaktion*, 10:353–402.

Jannik Strötgen and Michael Gertz. 2010. Heideltime: High quality rule-based extraction and normalization of temporal expressions. In *Proc. of the 5th International Workshop on Semantic Evaluation*, pages 321–324.

Detecting Visually Relevant Sentences for Fine-Grained Classification

Olivia Winn*, **Madhavan Kavanur Kidambi*** and **Smaranda Muresan**[†]
*Computer Science Department, Columbia University
[†] Center for Computational Learning Systems, Columbia University
olivia@cs.columbia.edu, mk3700@columbia.edu, smara@columbia.edu

Abstract

Detecting discriminative semantic attributes from text which correlate with image features is one of the main challenges of zero-shot learning for fine-grained image classification. Particularly, using full-length encyclopedic articles as textual descriptions has had limited success, one reason being that such documents contain many non-visual or unrelated sentences. We propose a method to automatically extract visually relevant sentences from Wikipedia documents. Our model, based on a convolutional neural network, is robustly tested through ground truth labeling obtained via Amazon Mechanical Turk, achieving 81.73% F1 measure.

1 Introduction

Current research in multimodal fusion and cross-modal mapping relies primarily on pre-aligned datasets of images and their short captions or tags, where the text is known to contain visually descriptive content directly related to its image (Baroni, 2016). These texts are usually manually collected, and restricted in length to words, phrases, and sentences. Using full-length documents such as Wikipedia articles would potentially allow automated access to already available rich descriptive content and would greatly aid the task of fine-grained classification across numerous domains, many of which have rich image datasets (such as birds (Welinder et al., 2010), flowers (Nilsback and Zisserman, 2008), aircraft (Maji et al., 2013), and dogs (Khosla et al., 2011).)

Unfortunately, most full-length documents contain predominantly non-visual text, making them noisy with respect to visual information and limiting the success of zero-shot learning techniques

```
...
Description
The Fish Crow is superficially similar to the American Crow but is
smaller and has a more silky plumage by comparison... The eyes are
dark brown...Fish crows tend to have more slender bills and feet.
There may also be a small sharp hook at the end of the upper bill..
[...]
Diet
Food is taken mainly from the ground and even in shallow water
where the bird will hover and pluck food items out of the water with
its feet. The fish crow is omnivorous. [...]
Breeding
The nest is usually built high in a tree and is often accompanied in
nearby trees with other nests of the same species forming small, loose
colonies. There are usually 4-5 eggs laid. Pale blue-green in colour,
they bear blotches of olive-brown.[...]
Conservation
This species appears to be somewhat more resistant to West Nile
Virus than the American crow. [...]
```

Figure 1: Example Sentences from Wikipedia article on the Fish Crow.

for fine-grained classification (Elhoseiny et al., 2013; Elhoseiny et al., 2015; Lei Ba et al., 2015). Furthermore, the visual portion of the text often describes objects outside the classifier's interest, such as the color of a bird's eggs when the task is identifying bird species (see Figure 1).

Thus, the question we address in this paper is as follows: can we *automatically identify visually descriptive sentences relevant to a particular object* from documents that may contain predominantly non-visual text? We refer to this type of sentence as 'visually relevant'. Answering this question would allow us to automatically build aligned datasets of images with rich sentence-level descriptions, removing the necessity of manually creating aligned image-text datasets.

In this work, we focus on bird species, as this is one of the most well-studied and challenging fine-grained classification domains, using Wikipedia articles as our text (Section 2). To build our computational models, we must first define the notion of 'visually relevant' sentences. We use the defini-

Proceedings of the 5th Workshop on Vision and Language, pages 86–91,
Berlin, Germany, August 12 2016. ©2016 Association for Computational Linguistics

tion of Visually Descriptive Language (VDL) introduced by Gaizauskas et al. (2015), with some restrictions. Like VDL, we aim to identify 'visually confirmed' rather than 'visually concrete' segments of text as our descriptions correspond to a class (the bird species) rather than a particular image. For example, a sentence describing a bird's feet can be a 'visually relevant' sentence for a bird, though it would not be 'visually concrete' for an image of the bird flying with its feet hidden. Unlike VDL, for the scope of this paper we are interested only in the sentences which are *visually descriptive with respect to the object (i.e., bird species)*. We define such sentences as containing *visually relevant language* (VRL).

To build our training data, we make a simplifying assumption: a sentence is only considered to contain visually relevant language if it is in the 'Description' section of the article. While other sections may contain visually descriptive language, we assume they describe other objects such as the eggs. This simplifying assumption allows us to approach our problem as a *sentence classification task* (is a sentence VRL or non-VRL), and provides an automatic, though noisy, approach for labeling the training data. We collect a dataset of 1150 Wikipedia articles about birds to train the non-linear, non-consecutive convolution neural network architecture proposed by Lei et al. (2015). The architecture of this particular CNN is well suited to model sentences in our corpus such as *"Adults have upperparts streaked with brown, grey, black and white"* as it captures non-consecutive grams such as *"upperparts brown"*, *"upperparts gray"*, *"streaked white"*, etc.

To test our model in a robust manner, we use crowdsourcing to manually annotate all sentences as either VRL or non-VRL from an unseen set of 200 Wikipedia articles (for a total of 6342 sentences) (Section 2), corresponding to the bird classes in the Caltech-UCSD Birds-200-2011 dataset (Welinder et al., 2010).

Our experiments show that the CNN model trained on the noisy VRL dataset performs very well when tested on a human-labeled VRL dataset: 83.4% Precision, 80.13% Recall, 81.73% F1 measure (Section 4). Our analysis highlights several findings: 1) VRL sentences outside of the description section, or in documents with no Description section, are properly labeled by the model as VRL; 2) non-VRL sentences within the Description sec-

	Training	Development
VRL	6355	794
non-VRL	27292	3411
Total	33647	4205

Table 1: Statistics of the Training and Dev. Sets

tion (many documents included descriptions of birdsong in these sections) are correctly labeled by the model as non-VRL (Section 4). The datasets, including the crowdsourcing annotations for the 200 documents are released to the research community (`http://github.com/oh-livia/VRL_Wiki_Dataset`). This dataset will be useful to advance research on fine-grained classification, given that the Caltech-UCSD Birds-200-2011 is one of the most highly used datasets for this task.

2 Datasets

To train our models we collected a set of 1150 Wikipedia articles of bird species. As a future goal of this work is to correlate the extracted textual information with image data, the training documents were specifically chosen not to correspond to the 200 birds species in the Caltech-UCSD Birds-200-11 dataset, which were set aside as test data. Of these 1150 documents, 690 of them contained sections labeled "Description" or related headings such as "Appearance", which allowed us to build our training and development sets. All sentences in the sections labeled "Description", "Appearance" and "Identification" were considered instances of the VRL class and everything else as instances of the non-VRL class; this labeling scheme we refer to as 'noisy'. Table 1 shows the statistics of the number of training and development instances used to build the computational models. The dataset is highly unbalanced: VRL sentences comprise 19% of both training and development. This skew is typical of many descriptive documents, and as such provides an appropriate model to train on.

To test our models we use the Wikipedia articles of the 200 birds in the Caltech-UCSD Birds-200-11 previously collected by Elhoseiny et al. (2013), consisting of 6342 sentences, which we call 200_{VRL}. To see whether our computational models trained on the noisy VRL dataset are able to detect VRL sentences as judged by humans, we conducted a crowdsourcing experiment.

2.1 Crowdsourcing to Annotate Sentences as Visually Relevant

We define a sentence-level annotation task, where each sentence in a document is assigned one of the following labels: **1** — the sentence contains visually relevant language (VRL), i.e. it is visually descriptive with respect to the object under consideration (birds species) (see examples (1) and (2)); and **0** — the sentence does not contain visually relevant language (see examples (3), (4), (5)).

Label **1** (VRL sentence) is assigned when the entire sentence is visually relevant (ex (1)) or when it is partially visually relevant (e.g., in example (2) only the underlined part is visually relevant):

(1) It has a black cap and a chestnut lower belly

(2) Males give increasingly vocal displays and show off the white markings of the wings in flight and of the tail [...]

Label **0** (non-VRL sentence) is assigned when the sentence describes the object of interest (bird species) but it is not visually descriptive (ex (3)), when it is visually descriptive but not relevant to the object (ex (4)), or when it is neither visually descriptive nor associated with the bird species.

(3) Males have 2 distinct types of songs - classified as short and long songs.

(4) The egg coloring is a brown spotted greenish-white.

(5) Finally volcanic eruptions on Torishima continues to be a threat.

In addition to the above labeling, for cases where a Turker chose the label **1** they were asked to provide information about the particular visually relevant text segments by specifying the *bird*, the *body part* and the *description*. While these phrase-level annotations are not used for our current task, they could be used in future work when joint-learning from text and images, especially to align information related to each body part of the bird. In addition, they could be used to build a graph-based representation of image descriptions similar to scene graphs (Schuster et al., 2015).

The annotation task was done at the sentence level and each sentence was annotated by three Turkers on Amazon Mechanical Turk. Besides the two labels **1** and **0**, the Turkers could also select "I don't know" and provide an explanation for why they could not determine whether or not the sentence contains VRL. We used highly skilled Turkers ($\geq$ 500 completed HITS and $\geq$ 95% approval rate) and we paid 5 cents per HIT (each HIT contained only one sentence). The inter-annotator agreement was very high, with a Fleiss $\mathcal{K}$ score of 0.8273. Only 8.64% of the sentences did not have a unanimous vote. Less than 2% of the sentences had at least one Turker vote 'I don't know'; of these, less than 0.05% garnered one vote each of **1**, **0** and 'I don't know'.

To build the test set for the computational models we use majority voting (at least two annotators selected the label). For the few cases where we did not have majority voting (0.05% of data) we selected the **0** label, as only one Turker voted **1** while the other two said **0** and 'I don't know'. This test set, which we call $\mathbf{200}_{HumVRL}$, contains 1248 sentences of class **1** (VRL) and 5094 sentences of class **0** (non-VRL).

3 Detecting Visually Relevant Sentences

As mentioned earlier, our task can be framed as a binary sentence classification problem, where each sentence is labeled either as VRL or non-VRL. Deep learning methods, and in particular convolutional neural networks (CNNs), have become some of the top performing methods on various NLP tasks that can be modeled as sentence classification (e.g, sentiment analysis, question type classification) (Kim, 2014; Kalchbrenner et al., 2014; Lei et al., 2015).

We use the non-linear, non-consecutive convolution neural network architecture proposed by Lei et al. (2015), which we refer to as $\mathbf{CNN}_{Lei}$. This CNN uses tensor products to combine non-consecutive n-grams of each sentence to create an embedding per sentence. The non-consecutive aspect of the n-gram allows it to capture co-occurrence of words spread across sentences: *"yellow crown, rump and flank patch"* will generate representations of the relevant noun-adjective pairs *"yellow crown"*, *"yellow rump"*, and *"yellow flank patch"*. The tensor product is used as a "generalized approach" to linear concatenation of the n-grams, as concatenation is "insufficient to directly capture relevant information in the n-gram" (Lei et al., 2015, p 1). We use the training and development set described in Table 1 that comes from the 690 documents with 'Description' headings.

Hyperparameters and Word Vectors. The word vectors are pre-trained on the entire set of 1150 Wikipedia articles about birds using the word2vec model of Mikolov et al. (2013) with a window context of 20 words and vectors of 150 dimensions. Notice that we do not use the documents in the test set 200_{VRL} for training the word vectors. We chose to use domain specific text to pre-train the word vectors in order to make sure we are capturing domain specific semantics such as proper word senses. Words such as "crown", when trained on a different corpus, would typically have an embedding very close to words such as "royalty", "tiara", etc; in the domain of bird descriptions, "crown" maps most closely to "feathers" and "head". The hyperparameters for the CNN model are: L2 regularization weight is 0.0001, n-gram order is 3 and hidden feature dimension is 50.

4 Experimental Setup and Results

Test Datasets. We first evaluate the $\mathbf{CNN}_{Lei}$ model on the 200_{HumVRL} dataset described in Section 2, which contains the 6342 sentences labeled by Turkers (class distribution: 1248 sentences in class **1** and 5094 sentences in class **0**). Since our computational model was trained on the noisy visually relevant sentences (where the labels were determined by the 'Description' section of the documents), we wanted to evaluate how the model performed on a similarly constructed test set. Thus, instead of considering the human labels for the 6342 sentences, a sentence was assigned to class **1** if it belonged to the Description, Appearance or Identification sections and to class **0** otherwise. We call this dataset $200_{NoisyVRL}$ (class distribution: 1258 sentences in class **1** and 5084 sentences in class **0**). Note that while it seems as if only 10 sentences changed, many of the sentences in the 'Description' sections were labeled by humans as class 0, and many sentences outside these sections labeled as class 1. However, one possible issue with the $200_{NoisyVRL}$ dataset is that some documents do not contain any description-type sections and thus all sentences are labeled **0**, which might affect measuring the performance of the model. Thus, we considered additional test sets containing only the documents that had sections labeled with 'Description', 'Appearance' or 'Identification' (142 documents out of the original 200 documents). Using these documents, we

constructed a dataset $142_{NoisyVRL}$, where class **1** contained sentences that were part of the three description-type sections, and class **0** contained all other sentences (class distribution: 1156 class **1** and 3836 class **0**). In addition, we also used the Turkers' labels (majority voting) for the corresponding sentences in these 142 documents. We call this dataset 142_{HumVRL} (class distribution: 992 class **1** and 4000 class **0**). Since the CNN model was trained on the noisy labeling, a reasonable assumption is that the classification results would be better on the $200_{NoisyVRL}$ and $142_{NoisyVRL}$ datasets than on the 200_{HumVRL} and 142_{HumVRL} datasets.

Baseline. As baseline, we used the same neural bag-of-words model (**nBoW**) as Lei et al. (2015). We use the same training and development sets as for the CNN model (Table 1), along with the same word embeddings.

Results and Discussion. Table 2 shows the results of the $\mathbf{CNN}_{Lei}$ model and the **nBoW** model on the four datasets. The CNN model performs slightly better than the baseline on all datasets in terms of F1 measure, with a much better Recall but worse Precision. Given that the end goal is to use the extracted visually relevant sentences together with images for fine-grained classification, and that the amount of visually relevant sentences in a document is small with respect to the document length, having high Recall is important.

One of the most interesting findings of this study is that both of the computational models perform much better on the human-labeled visually relevant datasets (200_{HumVRL}, 142_{HumVRL}) than on the noisy visually relevant datasets ($200_{NoisyVRL}$, $142_{NoisyVRL}$). In particular, the recall increases significantly (e.g., from 63.24% on $142_{NoisyVRL}$ to 80.15% on 142_{HumVRL} using the $\mathbf{CNN}_{Lei}$ model).

An error analysis highlights that the computational models are more 'conservative' with the classification of VRL than the noisy labeling. As mentioned earlier, the Description sections of the Wikipedia articles often (though not always) contain details pertaining to the birds' song. However, despite being trained on such a labeling, the computational models do not classify most sentences related primarily to the description of birds' song as VRL. This result was most likely aided by the fact that some of the training documents contain

Models	200_{HumVRL}			$200_{NoisyVRL}$			142_{HumVRL}			$142_{NoisyVRL}$		
	P(%)	R(%)	F(%)	P(%)	R(%)	F(%)	P(%)	R(%)	F(%)	P(%)	R(%)	F(%)
CNN$_{Lei}$	83.40	80.13	81.73	66.06	62.96	64.47	82.94	80.15	81.52	82.04	63.24	71.42
nBoW	88.61	73.56	80.39	67.31	55.33	60.73	88.48	73.32	80.19	84.11	55.88	67.15

Table 2: Classification results on the four datasets

song descriptions outside of the description-type sections, so the words pertaining to sound were not correlated as strongly with the VRL class. It is also possible that the abundance of appearance descriptions in each description section would encourage the visual words to have a much stronger effect on the 'visualness' of a sentence. One such example is the sentence *"The song is a series of musical notes which sound like: wheeta wheeta whee-tee-oh, for which a common pneumonic is 'The red, the red T-shirt'"*. Even the repetition of the word *'red'* is not enough to make the classifier label the sentence as VRL.

Another type of example that explains these results are sentences that describe the weight of the birds, such as *"Recorded weights range from 0.69 to 2 kg,[...]"* These sentences were part of the Description section, but were not marked as VRL by either the Turkers or the computational models.

We also analyzed some of the false positives of the **CNN**$_{Lei}$ model on the 142_{HumVRL} and 200_{HumVRL} datasets. One type of error comes from sentences that are visually descriptive, but not visually relevant, such as sentences that describe other objects like eggs. For example, the sentence *"The egg shells are of various shades of light or bluish grey with irregular, dark brown spots or greyish-brown splotches"* was labeled as VRL by the model but not by the Turkers. More interesting are the false positives that contain comparison words such as *"clapping or clicking has been observed more often in females than in males"*, and words having to do with appearance that do not specifically describe how the bird looks such as *"this bird is more often seen than heard"*.

5   Related Work

There are two lines of work most closely related to ours. First, Gaizauskas et al. (2015) propose a definition and typology of Visually Descriptive Language (VDL). They show that humans are able to reliably annotate text segments as containing 'visually descriptive' language or not, providing evidence that standalone text can be classified by the visualness of its contents. In our work, motivated by the end task of fine-grained classification, we restrict the definition to 'visually relevant'. As Gaizauskas et al. (2015) do, we show that humans can reliably annotate text as visually relevant or not. Unlike Gaizauskas et al. (2015), we propose a method to automatically detect visually relevant sentences from full-text documents. Second, Dodge et al. (2012) propose a method to separate visual text from non-visual text in image captions. However, their method focuses just on noun-phrases, while our approach finds visually relevant sentences in full-length documents.

While our end result is a set of visually relevant text descriptions, our approach is complementary to the rich body of work on generating text descriptions from images (see (Bernardi et al., 2016) for a survey), since our method *extracts such descriptions from existing text.*

6   Conclusion

Our work shows that it is possible to take domain-specific full-length documents—such as Wikipedia articles for birds species—and classify their sentences by visual relevancy using a CNN model trained on a noisy dataset. As many documents generally have a small proportion of visually relevant sentences, this approach automatically generates high quality visually relevant textual descriptions for images to be used by zero-shot learning approaches for fine-grained image classification tasks (e.g., (Wang et al., 2009)). While our study has focused on bird species, we believe that this method is generally applicable for other domains used in fine-grained classification research such as flowers and dogs (all have associated Wikipedia articles and Description/Appearance sections). In future work, we plan to use the outcomes of this work for joint learning from text and images.

Acknowledgments

This research was funded by the NSF (award IIS-409257). We thank the anonymous reviewers for helpful feedback.

References

M. Baroni. 2016. Grounding distributional semantics in the visual world. *Language and Linguistics Compass*, 10(1):3–13.

Raffaella Bernardi, Ruket Cakici, Desmond Elliott, Aykut Erdem, Erkut Erdem, Nazli Ikizler-Cinbis, Frank Keller, Adrian Muscat, and Barbara Plank. 2016. Automatic description generation from images: A survey of models, datasets, and evaluation measures. *Journal of Artificial Intelligence Research*, 55.

Jesse Dodge, Amit Goyal, Xufeng Han, Alyssa Mensch, Margaret Mitchell, Karl Stratos, Kota Yamaguchi, Yejin Choi, Hal Daumé III, Alexander C Berg, et al. 2012. Detecting visual text. In *Proceedings of the 2012 Conference of the North American Chapter of the Association for Computational Linguistics: Human Language Technologies*, pages 762–772. Association for Computational Linguistics.

Mohamed Elhoseiny, Babak Saleh, and Ahmed Elgammal. 2013. Write a classifier: Zero-shot learning using purely textual descriptions. In *Proceedings of the IEEE International Conference on Computer Vision*, pages 2584–2591.

Mohamed Elhoseiny, Ahmed Elgammal, and Babak Saleh. 2015. Tell and predict: Kernel classifier prediction for unseen visual classes from unstructured text descriptions. *IEEE Conference on Computer Vision and Pattern Recognition Workshops (CVPR)*.

Robert Gaizauskas, Josiah Wang, and Arnau Ramisa. 2015. Defining visually descriptive language. In *Proceedings of the 2015 Workshop on Vision and Language (VL15): Vision and Language Integration Meets Cognitive Systems*.

Nal Kalchbrenner, Edward Grefenstette, and Phil Blunsom. 2014. A convolutional neural network for modelling sentences. In *Proceedings of the 52nd Annual Meeting of the Association for Computational Linguistics, ACL 2014, June 22-27, 2014, Baltimore, MD, USA, Volume 1: Long Papers*, pages 655–665.

Aditya Khosla, Nityananda Jayadevaprakash, Bangpeng Yao, and Li Fei-Fei. 2011. Novel dataset for fine-grained image categorization. In *First Workshop on Fine-Grained Visual Categorization, IEEE Conference on Computer Vision and Pattern Recognition*, Colorado Springs, CO, June.

Yoon Kim. 2014. Convolutional neural networks for sentence classification. *Proceedings of the 2014 Conference on Empirical Methods in Natural Language Processing (EMNLP)*, pages 1746–1751.

Jimmy Lei Ba, Kevin Swersky, Sanja Fidler, et al. 2015. Predicting deep zero-shot convolutional neural networks using textual descriptions. In *Proceedings of the IEEE International Conference on Computer Vision*, pages 4247–4255.

Tao Lei, Regina Barzilay, and Tommi Jaakkola. 2015. Molding cnns for text: Non-linear, non-consecutive convolutions. In *Proceedings of the 2015 Conference on Empirical Methods in Natural Language Processing (EMNLP)*.

S. Maji, J. Kannala, E. Rahtu, M. Blaschko, and A. Vedaldi. 2013. Fine-grained visual classification of aircraft. Technical report.

Tomas Mikolov, Ilya Sutskever, Kai Chen, Greg Corrado, and Jeffrey Dean. 2013. Distributed representations of words and phrases and their compositionality. *Advances in Neural infgormation Processing Systems*, pages 3111–3119.

M-E. Nilsback and A. Zisserman. 2008. Automated flower classification over a large number of classes. In *Proceedings of the Indian Conference on Computer Vision, Graphics and Image Processing*, Dec.

Sebastian Schuster, Ranjay Krishna, Angel Chang, Li Fei-Fei, and Christopher D Manning. 2015. Generating semantically precise scene graphs from textual descriptions for improved image retrieval. In *Proceedings of the Fourth Workshop on Vision and Language*, pages 70–80.

Josiah Wang, Katja Markert, and Mark Everingham. 2009. Learning models for object recognition from natural language descriptions. In *British Machine Vision Conference (BMVC)*, volume 1, page 2.

P. Welinder, S. Branson, T. Mita, C. Wah, F. Schroff, S. Belongie, and P. Perona. 2010. Caltech-UCSD Birds 200. Technical Report CNS-TR-2010-001, California Institute of Technology.